THE SECRET TECHNIQUES OF
BONSAI

THE SECRET TECHNIQUES OF BONSAI

A guide to starting, raising, and shaping bonsai

Masakuni Kawasumi II
WITH MASAKUNI KAWASUMI III

TRANSLATED BY **Kay Yokota**
COLOR PHOTOGRAPHY BY **Yasuo Saji**

KODANSHA USA

Pages 2–3: Ezo spruce (*Picea jezoensis*), 420 years (70 years as a bonsai
   after being collected from the wild), 31 inches (80 cm)
Pages 6–7: Trident maple (*Acer buergerianum*), 70 years (after group
   planting), 22 inches (55 cm)

Black-and-white photography: Yasuo Saji, pp. 13, 25 (center), 28 (bottom two),
45. All other photos by the authors.

Line drawings by Tadamitsu Omori

Published by Kodansha USA Publishing
451 Park Avenue South
New York, NY 10016

Distributed in the United Kingdom and continental Europe by Kodansha Europe
Ltd.

Printed in South Korea through Dai Nippon Printing Co., Ltd.
ISBN-978-1-56836-543-5

First edition published in Japan in 2005 by Kodansha International
First US edition 2013 by Kodansha USA, an imprint of Kodansha USA Publishing
24 23 22 21 20 19   10 9 8 7 6 5 4

www.kodanshausa.com

CONTENTS

Introducing the Latest Bonsai Techniques to Enthusiasts Worldwide

Japanese culture has become a highly important subject of study around the world. Of the numerous cultural traditions of Japan, bonsai in particular is an art that has attracted the interest of students of Japanese culture, and especially of plant enthusiasts, for the singular method by which trees and shrubs are grown. People the world over are taking up bonsai cultivation with extraordinary passion, and the pace at which they are doing so is nothing short of astounding. Why has bonsai come to enjoy such attention and adoration? Surely it is because it has a magical, heart-grabbing appeal that is not to be found in regular gardening.

For over three decades, I have been traveling abroad nearly every year to places like the United States, Canada, Australia, and countries in Europe and Southeast Asia to see the bonsai specimens cultivated there. The skills of bonsai enthusiasts in these countries have improved with the passing years, and the progress they have made is phenomenal. In particular, I have witnessed many impressive bonsai of indigenous species that have been successfully cultivated to suit the local climate. I would like to take this opportunity to pay tribute to the ardor and hard work with which the enthusiasts of each country have heightened their bonsai skills.

Based on my encounters with a large number of bonsai worldwide and my fifty-plus years of experience in bonsai cultivation, in this volume I will go a step further than in my previous book, *Bonsai with American Trees*, and guide you through the latest cultivation techniques, explaining how to use bonsai tools to their full advantage. The techniques also amply incorporate the advice of my son, a professional tree doctor. I am confident that anyone, regardless of their level, will easily be able to produce splendid specimens by practicing the techniques presented in this book.

The art of bonsai originated in China some 1,700 years ago, around the end of the Han Dynasty, and was introduced to Japan in the latter days of the Heian period (794–1185). The art was influenced by the climate and environment, national character, tree species, and other considerations, and today enthusiasts worldwide acknowledge Japan as the home of bonsai. Needless to say, the modern development and advancement of bonsai art in

Japan in the Taisho era (1912–26) and Showa era (1926–89) is due to the diligence and hard work of many bonsai specialists. At the same time, however, it is said that bonsai would not have been able to progress as it has without the wide array of specialized bonsai tools that were invented and developed following the creation of the first bonsai shears by Masakuni Kawasumi I (1880–1950) in the early Showa era.

Over the years, these tools have gradually come into widespread use by bonsai cultivators worldwide. Nevertheless, most of the books that have been written by specialists thus far say very little about the correct use of these tools in actual bonsai work—for instance, how you can use the tools to work effectively, in which ways your efficiency will improve, and what results you can expect. Bonsai enthusiasts—particularly those outside Japan—have long been kept waiting for a detailed commentary on bonsai techniques based on the appropriate use of tools.

Bonsai is said to be a living art, and the tools need to be selected according to the growth and condition of the tree. By using your tools wisely, you will be able to further enhance the splendor of your bonsai with little time and effort, as well as make them more manageable. When humans undergo an operation, surgeons choose from a variety of instruments, such as surgical knives, forceps, and tweezers, according to the part of the body and the ailment. The use of tools for operating on bonsai should be approached

Masakuni Kawasumi I, ca. 1930s.

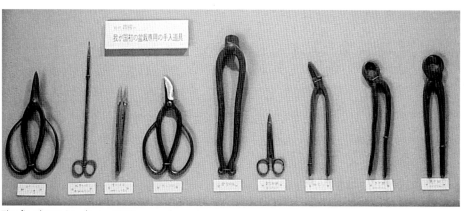

The first bonsai tools, ca. 1928.

in the same manner as the use of surgical instruments on the human body. It is by selecting good tools that best suit the task at hand and using them appropriately that you will reap the greatest benefits from any bonsai procedure.

He who loves bonsai possesses a heart that loves peace. The living art of bonsai is the very symbol of peace, and the act of cultivating bonsai leads directly to a love of peace. I hope bonsai enthusiasts around the world find this volume of assistance in further developing their cultivation skills.

I hereby pray for a bright century of world peace and for further progress in the international world of bonsai.

Masakuni Kawasumi II

The above was written by my father, Masakuni II, who passed away in the summer of 2002 with the manuscript and photographs for this book eighty percent completed. Having studied bonsai under his tutelage since my childhood, I succeeded to the name of Masakuni and set myself to finishing the book, which has reached publication at last.

I also pray, as did my late father, for a bright century of world peace and for further progress in the international world of bonsai.

Masakuni Kawasumi III
Tree Doctor

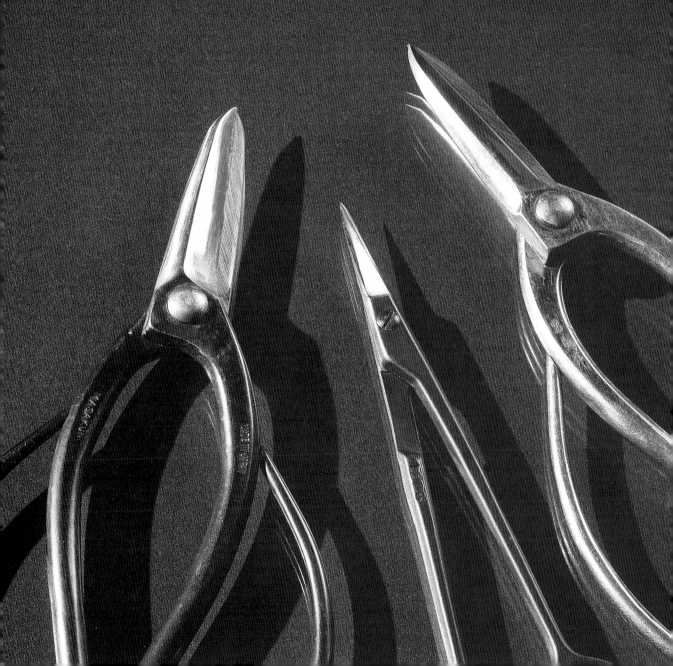

Part *1*
THE BASICS

Before Getting Started

The following chapters explore the actual art of cultivating bonsai. Before moving on, however, there are several facts that I would like readers to know. It is to be hoped that the discussion will help guide you in your approach to the care of bonsai.

The variety of plants on the Earth are said to number in the hundreds of thousands. While the common names of the plants differ in many countries, the species to which they belong have universally recognized names, which are all in Latin. These Latin names are also used in the world of bonsai. But perhaps because botanists worldwide recognize Japan as the home of the art, bonsai is known across the globe by its Japanese name. People of every country will know what a bonsai is without being told that it is a "miniature potted tree" or "dwarfed potted plant." Nowadays the term "bonsai" has gained universal currency.

There is another traditional Japanese art that concerns itself with plant life: ikebana. It was once far more popular in the West than bonsai. But today, many people overseas are not familiar with the word "ikebana," which often must be explained as meaning the "Japanese art of flower arrangement."

Why has bonsai surpassed ikebana to win the same degree of truly worldwide acceptance; as have Zen, judo, and karate? I would like to explore this question before moving on to the fundamental issue of what bonsai is.

><

Today, a great number of people around the world have developed a profound interest in the cultural traditions of Japan and are conducting studies of diverse Japanese arts. Moreover, the development of modern industry has led to a global increase in leisure time, so that people now devote more time than ever to various diversions. Along with these changes, the very nature of pastimes is being transformed in every country. In days past, the most popular pastimes were of the passive kind, such as watching movies or listening to music. These days, however, more active, creative pastimes that involve actual doing or the making of things are finding favor.

The cultivation of bonsai appears to have gained popularity as one such creative pastime. But bonsai is more than just another hobby or form of entertainment to occupy one's spare time—it has a spiritual aspect on a far higher plane than can be found in most other leisure activities. That, it seems to me, is why people the world over have

By vigilantly watching over the growth of your precious plants, they will respond to your loving care.
Ezo spruce (*Picea jezoensis*), 50 years (after layering), 18 inches (45 cm)

lately come to take such zealous interest in the art.

Ikebana and bonsai, while both hailing from the cultural traditions of Japan, stand in stark contrast to one another in that one is static and the other dynamic. The student of ikebana is instructed to arrange flowers with the heart. As soon as the flowers have been arranged in a vessel, an ikebana is suspended in a still reflection of the artist's state of mind at that moment in time. By contrast, a bonsai embodies a daily continuum of life, and its cultivator can observe subtle day-to-day changes in the plant over a long period of time.

The world of ikebana has numerous schools, each characterized by a traditional *iemoto* system: to this day, the schools maintain a hierarchical structure whereby the *iemoto*, or master, confers a certificate as a student attains a new level of mastery. Each school has a unique style of arranging flowers, moreover, and students must adhere strictly to the traditional forms of their respective schools.

Meanwhile, bonsai styles are based only on the natural shapes of trees, and there are no rigorous rules dictating how a bonsai must be sculpted. A bonsai needs just a small amount of human help so that it can grow in the image of the same species in its natural state. Of course, to keep it from growing in an unattractive manner, the tree at times may need to be restrained if it behaves willfully and insists, for instance, on extending a branch too far. Stroking the tip of the branch with the fingers will stimulate ethylene production and halt the branch's growth. It is important to make regular rounds of the nursery, looking out for changes in each tree, so that they develop into the bonsai you envision. By vigilantly watching over the growth of your precious plants, they will respond to your loving care.

Curiously enough, bonsai will begin to reflect—though very gradually—the mind of their cultivator, eventually taking on the very character of that person. If the cultivator is crude, the bonsai will come to mirror that crudeness. If the cultivator is a refined person of integrity, the bonsai will come to exhibit that refinement. More than anything else, I believe it is this fascinating spiritual potential that has set bonsai clearly apart from ikebana and allowed it to take root around the world.

Finally, we reach the question of what bonsai is. In order to know the answer, we must consider its essence and how it differs from ordinary potted plants.

As I wrote earlier, the word bonsai has nowadays gained universal currency. But even in Japan, which is recognized by all as the home of the art, there still are people who cannot tell bonsai from other potted plants. In fact, quite a few people think that any plant in a pot is a bonsai. This, however, is not true. I would also note that there are other types of cultivated plants similar to bonsai, such as *bonkei* (tray landscapes) and *hakoniwa* (miniature landscapes).

In contemplating the distinction between bonsai and these other types of plants, I suggest the following definition: bonsai are trees and/or shrubs cultivated in a pot in a style that (1) evokes images of the trees and/or shrubs in nature, or (2) moves the hearts of viewers. Thus, a plant that has been nurtured in a pot for many years cannot be called a bonsai if it does not satisfy either definition, while a plant that has been cultivated for only a short period can nonetheless be called a bonsai if it does. For example, if a flowering tree is reared in a pot just to appreciate its blossoms or view its fruit, it will not qualify as a bonsai, no matter the number of years or decades that pass. On the other hand, picture a tree that has survived decades or centuries of severe climatic conditions in the wild and metamorphosed into an awe-inspiring figure: its trunk roughened and gnarled; some of its branches broken midway and lifeless at the ends; and highlights of naturally formed bone-white deadwood, known as *jin*. Such a tree will become a bonsai the instant it is potted, regardless of the length of time it has been cultivated.

Furthermore, those trees and plants from which emanate the merest aura of *wabi* (quiet refinement) or *sabi* (timeworn elegance) are bonsai in a deeper sense of the word. Indeed, expressing *wabi* and *sabi* in plants is the ultimate ideal of bonsai cultivation.

This approach to bonsai reflects the strong influence of the supreme goal of Zen Buddhism—one of the religions brought to Japan between the end of the Heian period (794–1185) and the Kamakura period (1185–1333)—namely, to steady and concentrate the mind. Among the bonsai kept at the Imperial Palace is a Japanese white pine said to have been cherished by Iemitsu, the third Tokugawa shogun, and now over four centuries old. There also are tiny bonsai that are small enough to sit in the palm of the hand yet live close to a century. These bonsai naturally evoke a sense of *wabi* and *sabi* in the eyes of every viewer. As well as being an art of expressing nature, bonsai is an art of time that holds a lofty spirituality.

PAGE **18** (CLOCKWISE FROM TOP LEFT): **Literati Style**, Japanese red pine (*Pinus densiflora*), 130 years (from seedling), 35 inches (90 cm). **Split-Trunk Style**, Japanese apricot (*Prunus mume*), 80 years (from seedling), 31 inches (80 cm). **Windswept Style**, Japanese red pine (*Pinus densiflora*), 50 years (from seedling), 20 inches (50 cm). **Slanting Style**, Ezo spruce (*Picea jezoensis*), 70 years (wild seedling), 31 inches (80 cm). **Informal Upright Style**, *Nishikigi* (a type of spindle tree, *Euonymus alatus*), 40 years (from cutting), 37 inches (95 cm).

PAGE **19** (CLOCKWISE FROM TOP LEFT): **Twin-Trunk Style**, Trident maple (*Acer buergerianum*), 30 years (from seedling), 28 inches (70 cm). **Semi-Cascade Style**, *Teika-kazura* (a type of star jasmine, *Trachelospermum asiaticum*), 15 years (from cutting), 12 inches (30 cm). **Rock-Grown Style**, Trident maple (*Acer buergerianum*), 80 years (with rock), 22 inches (55 cm).

CHAPTER 2

Species and Styles of Bonsai

Bonsai Species

Almost any plant can be made into a bonsai. But those with leaves that are particularly large and hard to miniaturize, such as the longleaf pine (*Pinus palustris*), the horse chestnut (*Aesculus hippocastanum*), and plane trees (genus *Platanus*), are believed to be unsuitable for bonsai. Moreover, since every tree has a different disposition, the manner of branching, the properties of the leaves, or other features of one tree may be better for a bonsai than those of another, even within the same species. Take care to pick out a promising specimen with which you believe you can create a masterpiece.

Trees are highly adaptable to new environments and can often be grown far from their native habitats. There are limitations, however, if they are being cultivated out of doors, and it is far easier to grow and care for species that are well adjusted to the local climate.

Conifers have been the most popular subjects of bonsai for ages, and masterpieces of these species can be found in many countries. In the future, as more and more bonsai are created with plants native to their respective countries, I predict that the art will undergo true internationalization, and interaction will deepen among bonsai cultivators of the world.

Bonsai Styles

Bonsai can be trained into a variety of shapes. In every instance, though, the basic idea is to grow the tree in a shape that clearly keeps to the natural form of that species. The art of bonsai has traditionally had basic styles, all reflecting the appearances of trees in nature. Today there are rare instances of specimens that have been excessively altered, or avant-garde specimens of which there is no likeness in nature. These should be regarded as exceptions to the rule, and bonsai enthusiasts are advised to look to the natural shapes of trees when starting a new bonsai.

Meanwhile, with some species, it is considered not unnatural to model them after other species. A typical example is the *satsuki* azalea (*Rhododendron indicum*). In the wild, *satsuki* shrubs grow in the *kabudachi* style, in which multiple trunks spring up from the same roots. But as they easily produce buds anywhere on their trunks and branches, which can then be used to fashion the shrubs freely into diverse shapes, it has become customary to train *satsuki* into styles that are characteristic of conifers or of other deciduous plants.

In this chapter, I introduce the principal styles of bonsai, along with the species that are commonly cultivated in each style. As I have observed from studying bonsai books and photograph collections published worldwide, it is becoming popular in America, Europe, and elsewhere to use the Japanese names of bonsai styles rather than their English counterparts. Here, for your reference, however, I have included the names in both languages.

Formal Upright Style, Japanese white pine.

Chokkan
Formal Upright Style

Chokkan, one of the most basic bonsai styles, is characterized by a trunk that shoots straight up from base to apex. Large trees of the plains often take this shape. The perfect *chokkan* bonsai has a gracefully tapering main trunk with roots spreading in all directions, its alternately arranged branches growing thinner and shorter in proportion to the trunk as they approach the top. It is a very stable shape that is common among conifers and many other species of trees. By their nature, the cryptomeria (*Cryptomeria japonica*) and Japanese cypress (*Chamaecyparis obtusa*) can also be cultivated in this shape without difficulty.

Shakan
Slanting Style
See photograph on page 18

Shakan is a style in which the trunk grows diagonally up. In natural settings, it is seen in trees growing on windy beaches, mountainsides, or mountaintops. The trunk may be slanted and straight, or it may have curves. Conifers are frequently grown in this shape.

Bunjin
Literati Style
See photograph on page 18

The *bunjin* bonsai has a distinctive spatial form: the trunk is thin relative to the tree's height, with sparse, gentle curves. The branches are few and short and grow only in the upper reaches, making the tree look tall. Twin-trunk and triple-trunk trees that are trained in this shape are also called *bunjin* bonsai. The style works well with species that have an air of softness, such as the red pine (*Pinus densiflora*).

Moyogi
Informal Upright Style
See photograph on page 18

The *moyogi* bonsai has a sinuous trunk. Natural curves in the tree may be used to create this shape, or the trunk may be deliberately bent. The focal point of this style is the contour and flow of the trunk. *Moyogi* is the most common style in bonsai and is suitable for conifers, the *satsuki* azalea, and numerous other plants.

CLOCKWISE FROM NEAR RIGHT:
Zelkova (*Zelkova serrata*),
95 years, 43 inches (110 cm)

Trident maple (*Acer buergerianum*), 40 years (with rock),
30 inches (75 cm)

Persimmon (*Diospyros kaki*),
70 years (from seedling),
24 inches (60 cm)

Orange (*Citrus*), 60 years
(from seedling), 10 inches
(25 cm)

Fukinagashi
Windswept Style

See photograph on page 18

The *fukinagashi* style is seen in pines and other trees that grow in places where strong winds blow in the same direction year-round, such as beaches. Every branch flows with the wind, from base to tip. The trunk is usually also slanted in the direction of the wind, but some *fukinagashi* bonsai have upright trunks, with just the branches seemingly drifting off in one direction.

Kengai
Cascade Style

Kengai is a style in which the trunk and branches lean far to the side and cascade to a level lower than the tree's base. Conifers growing in valleys and on rocky cliffs often take this shape.

Hankengai
Semi-Cascade Style

As with the *kengai* style, the trunk and branches of a *hankengai* bonsai extend out and down, the difference being that the tip of the tree does not hang lower than its base.

Bankan
Twisted-Trunk Style

The *bankan* style aptly represents the weather-beaten features of a tree that has grown in a harsh climate. The *bankan* bonsai typically does not grow very tall, and the curves of the trunk are far more pronounced than those of a *moyogi* bonsai. The trunk often is severely twisted or has turned into a *sabamiki* (split trunk), with parts of it withered to a bone white—a condition called *jin*. This style is especially favored for the sargent juniper (*Juniperus chinensis*).

Sabamiki
Split-Trunk Style

See photograph on page 18

The deadwood of a trunk is called *saba*. The *sabamiki* bonsai has a largely withered trunk, frequently coupled with partially withered branches that exhibit the bone-white features of *jin*. While conifers such as the sargent juniper are the primary species of choice for this style, there are also many fine *sabamiki* specimens of other trees—such as aged Japanese apricot (*Prunus mume*).

Cascade Style, *Isozansho* (an evergreen shrub of the *Rosaleae*).

Semi-Cascade Style, Sargent juniper.

Twisted-Trunk Style, Sargent juniper.

Neagari
Exposed-Root Style

Distinguished by roots that rise up high into the air, the *neagari* bonsai is made in the likeness of trees with roots that have become exposed due to the surface soil having been washed away by heavy weather. The bare roots have lignified and firmly anchor the tree. Many specimens of this style grasp rock between their roots, and may also be classified as *ishitsuki* (rock-grown) bonsai. Conifers, as well as maples, which form beautiful woody roots, are easily trained into this shape.

Hokidachi
Broom Style

The *hokidachi* bonsai resembles a broom standing on its handle, with a profusion of branches neatly radiating upward from a trunk that stands erect from the roots. The species best suited for the *hokidachi* style is the zelkova (*Zelkova serrata*), which naturally grows in this shape. There are also occasional instances of the Chinese hackberry (*Celtis sinensis*) being cultivated in this style.

Shidare
Weeping Style

Drooping branches characterize the *shidare* bonsai. The style may be selected for the tamarisk (*Tamarix chinensis*), or for trees like the weeping willow (*Salix babylonica*) and weeping cherry (*Prunus Itosakura*), which, as their names suggest, have naturally weeping branches. It is a distinctive style that takes advantage of the trees' natural properties.

Sokan
Twin-Trunk Style *See photograph on page 19*

The *sokan* bonsai has a pair of trunks growing either from the same base or close to one another. The aesthetic focus is on the contrast and balance between the thicknesses and heights of the two trunks, which often are straight. Depending on the balance, the trunks may be called parent and child, husband and wife, or siblings. Trees preferred for this style include conifers, such as pines, the cryptomeria, and the Japanese cypress; and deciduous trees, such as maples.

Sankan
Triple-Trunk Style

The *sankan* bonsai has three trunks that are cultivated to slightly contrasting thicknesses and heights. The style is frequently employed with deciduous trees, such as maples.

Broom Style, Zelkova.

Weeping Style, *Shidare-zakura* (a type of Japanese cherry).

Triple-Trunk Style, *Yama-momiji* (a type of Japanese maple).

Gokan, Nanakan
Five-Trunk Style, Seven-Trunk Style

Bonsai with a multitude of trunks are usually designed to have an odd number of trunks, perhaps reflecting the preference in Eastern thought for odd numbers over even numbers. *Gokan* (five trunks) and *nanakan* (seven trunks) refer to those bonsai with distinct, countable trunks, each of which has a stronger presence than the trunks of a *kabudachi* bonsai (see next entry). Both coniferous and deciduous trees may be cultivated in these styles.

Kabudachi
Multiple-Trunk Style

Bonsai with five or more trunks arising from the same roots are collectively called *kabudachi* bonsai. The individual trunks should be grown to different thicknesses and heights to achieve an overall effect of either a small forest or a single tree. The zelkova (*Zelkova serrata*) and other deciduous trees are commonly grown in this style.

Yoseue
Group-Planting Style

In the *yoseue* style, trees of staggered sizes are planted together in the image of a grove or forest, and the bonsai is appreciated for its overall landscape. Trees of a single species are usually used, but occasionally different species are mixed together. To create an expansive landscape, *yoseue* bonsai are best made in an oblong, shallow pot or on a slab of rock.

With the exception of vines, any species—evergreen or deciduous—can be used to make *yoseue* bonsai. Moreover, specimens that would not look good standing alone, such as those with the roots or branches growing mostly on one side, often make fine material for group planting. *Yoseue* is a style that strongly reflects the aesthetic taste of the cultivator. I encourage you to give free rein to your creativity as you put together a *yoseue* bonsai of your preferred species in a pot of your choice.

Ikadabuki
Raft Style

To make an *ikadabuki* bonsai, a tree that has many horizontal branches growing on one side of the trunk is planted laterally in the soil, like a fallen tree with its branches pointing up. The upright limbs produce the effect of a group planting, or *yoseue*. This technique is rarely used nowadays, as it does not readily lend itself to creating depth.

Netsuranari
Sinuous-Root Style

The *netsuranari* bonsai resembles a *yoseue* bonsai, but all the trunks are connected by a single root system. It consists of a primary tree with multiple

Five-Trunk Style, *Yama-momiji*, (a type of Japanese maple).

Seven-Trunk Style, *Yama-momiji*, (a type of Japanese maple).

Multiple-Trunk Style, Zelkova.

Group-Planting Style, Japanese Judas Tree.

stems, each of which has emerged from various points of the sprawling roots and grown into a tree. Bonsai of this style are popularly created using the Japanese white pine (*Pinus parviflora*) or the Ezo spruce (*Picea jezoensis*) and are highly prized in Japan as auspicious trees.

Ishitsuki
Rock-Grown Style

All bonsai grown on rock are called *ishitsuki* bonsai, of which there are broadly three types. In each type, the rock is a major highlight.

Exposed roots grasping the rock. The rock is partially embedded in the soil of a pot. The long roots spread over the rock as if to embrace it, with most of the roots exposed except at the ends, where they reach into the soil. Over time the bare roots will fatten and lignify, filling up the space that initially existed between them and the rock and firmly clinging to it. The trident maple (*Acer buergerianum*) is favored for this style due to the beauty of the woody surface of its roots. A period of preparation is needed prior to making a bonsai of this style, as the roots of the tree to be used must have extended a long way.

Planted in hollows on the rock surface. The rock is laid either longitudinally or laterally, depending on its shape, and one tree or several trees are planted in soil that has been set in the hollows of the rock. The bonsai presents an image of trees growing on craggy mountains. The roots will usually remain attached to the rock, which is commonly placed in a water basin without soil. Often, this type of *ishitsuki* bonsai is made with a conifer trained in the *moyogi* or *kengai* style.

Planted in soil placed on a slab. The tree is planted in a mound of soil that sits on a thin, flat piece of rock. A variety of species both deciduous and evergreen are used—sometimes solo, depending on the size of the rock and the tree, but usually as a group planting. Thin, curved slabs may also be used; for this purpose, single *moyogi* trees, whether deciduous or evergreen, are said to be best.

Exposed roots grasping the rock. Trident maple.

Planted in hollows on the rock surface. Japanese white pine.

Planted in soil placed on a slab. Beech.

OTHER STYLES

The variations of the basic styles outlined above are numerous. There are specimens that combine two or three styles and cannot be clearly defined as exclusively belonging to any one style. In addition, there are specimens that radically diverge from the basic styles—such as bonsai with many sinuous limbs growing from the roots like an octopus spreading its tentacles, or bonsai that have been trained into highly artificial shapes. These instances, however, are few and far between.

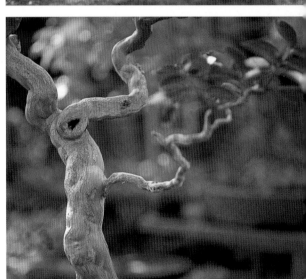

In the preceding pages I have described the principal styles of bonsai. The best way for the general enthusiast to enjoy the art of bonsai, I believe, is to use trees that are native to the locality and cultivate them in a naturally compatable style. Although with improved skill you may be able to mold trees into peculiar shapes, problems will arise over the long run if the shape is incompatible with the physiology and nature of the tree. Rather than shaping it forcibly, the road to a good bonsai is to let the tree grow freely and comfortably by harnessing the natural characteristics of the species and the individual tree. After all, it is the tree itself and not its cultivator that does the growing and shaping. We need to always remember that humans can only help that growth.

The Front of the Bonsai and Harmony with the Pot

There is one important point that should be noted in connection with bonsai forms, and that is the front of the bonsai. The front is where the tree appears the most attractive— the angle that best brings out the beauty of the tree's features, such as the contour of the trunk and the shape of the branches. In growing a bonsai of any style, it is important that the cultivator recognize the front of the tree from the time it is potted.

The bonsai pot has a front as well. A bonsai is correctly planted when the front of the tree matches the front of the pot, and it should be viewed from that angle. The pot should be selected for its balance with the tree. When the tree and the pot are in perfect harmony, each complementing the beauty and charm of the other, the bonsai is said to have "good *hachiutsuri*."

Masakuni II grew this bonsai from a seedling, shaping and tending it for over 40 years.
Chinese hackberry, *Celtis sinensis*, 43 years, 39 inches (100 cm)

CHAPTER 3
Starting a Bonsai

Obtaining new plants for bonsai is very exciting, not only for someone who is just about to start cultivating the first bonsai but equally for an enthusiast with many years of experience in the art. It brings with it the anticipation of the bonsai masterpiece that the plant may one day become.

The easiest way to start a new bonsai is to buy a semifinished specimen. In this chapter, though, I will primarily discuss methods by which you can produce your own potential bonsai. You may choose any of these methods according to your preference or purpose, but each has its advantages and difficulties. Be sure to have a good grasp of all the factors involved so that you can obtain the best material possible.

Misho

Growing from Seed

Although growing a bonsai from seed—a process called *misho*—takes some time, it is the easiest and surest way of creating your own bonsai. It is a joy to sow the seeds and watch them spring forth with life. There is also the satisfaction of creating a bonsai of your desired shape entirely from scratch. Seedlings of any species can be grown in large quantities, and you can then experience the thrill of picking out the seedlings that look the most promising.

SEEDING

The seeds for bonsai are sown in much the same way as the seeds of ordinary plants and flowers. Line the bottom of a shallow pot or a planter with soil and even out the surface. Place the seeds in the soil about 1 ¼ inches (3 cm) apart, then sprinkle over enough soil to cover the seeds. Water-retentive soil that has been sieved to a grain size of ⅛ inch (3 mm) or less should be used. Soak the seeds in water overnight prior to planting, and sow only those that have sunk to the bottom. Seeds that float to the surface of the water should not be planted, as they are highly unlikely to sprout.

After the seeds have been planted, place the seedbed in a sunny spot and water it regularly, taking care that the topsoil does not dry out.

SEEDING

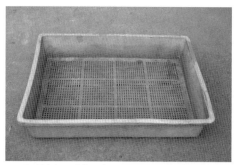

STEP 1. These zelkova (*Zelkova serrata*) seeds have been soaked in water overnight. Sow only those seeds that rest at the bottom, discarding those floating on the surface. (Do not soak the seeds for more than one night, or the germination rate will drop.)

STEP 2. This broad, flat planter can accommodate a large number of seedlings. The fine holes at the bottom measure only about ¹⁄₁₂ inch (2 mm) across.

STEP 3. Cover the bottom with evenly spread coarse soil with grains measuring ¹⁄₅ inch (5 mm) or more. This will ensure drainage and keep the planting soil from washing away.

STEP 4. Over the coarse soil add fine planting soil (*akadama* soil) that has been passed through a sieve with a ¹⁄₈-inch (3-mm) mesh. Remove fine pow soil particles of up to about ¹⁄₂₄ inch (1 mm) from the planting soil before adding it to the planter.

STEP 5. Even out the surface. The seedbed is now ready for planting.

STEP 6. Carefully place the seeds on the surface, one by one, using tweezers. The seeds should be about 1 ¼ inches (3 cm) apart.

STEP 7. Once the seeds have been laid out, sprinkle just enough planting soil to cover them. Using a sieve will allow you to sprinkle the soil evenly.

STEP 8. With a watering can, generously water the seedbed with a fine spray, taking care not to wash away the seeds. Continue the watering until the water coming out from the bottom of the planter is clear and free of impurities. The powdered soil will have been rinsed away from the planting soil. Place the planter in a warm, sunny place and keep watering it as the topsoil dries while you wait for the seeds to sprout.

AFTER SPROUTING

Seeds sown in spring will usually sprout within one or two months. The seeds of some coniferous trees, meanwhile, may stay dormant if the preceding winter was not cold enough and germinate only in the second or third year. In the case of such a species, do not lose hope if no shoots appear in the first month or two. Patiently continue watering the seedbed, watching carefully for signs of change.

After germination, not all the seedlings will grow equally well. Some will show slower growth, and should be removed. Even though they may have been lucky enough to sprout, such seedlings have little chance of survival. By removing them, the remaining seedlings will be able to receive more even and abundant sunlight.

In roughly two or three months the true leaves will have grown out fully. Around this time, trim the taproot growing straight downward to a length of about ½ inch (1 cm) and replant the seedlings in the shallowest available pot. Trimming the taproot at the time of the first repotting is essential, as it encourages the growth of lateral roots from around the base of the stem and prepares the plant for healthy root development. A long taproot that is left intact will grow even sturdier, with additional roots extending only from that one root, and very few lateral roots will develop. It will then become difficult to encourage surface roots to develop and radiate evenly from the trunk in all directions—the ideal root structure, known as *happo nebari*.

For a young seedling, trimming the taproot is a major operation, thus always use sharp shears so as not to damage the delicate tissue.

Many long lateral roots will have developed around the base by about two months after repotting. Begin feeding the seedlings diluted liquid fertilizer twice a month from around this time. In the following spring, replant in separate nursery pots the seedlings that you expect to raise as individual bonsai. When repotting, spread out the lateral roots growing near the base of the stem as evenly as possible in all directions to form the basis for a radial root structure.

This point marks the beginning of the real process of crafting a bonsai, which I discuss starting in Chapter 4.

On the opposite page are photographs of the seeds of common bonsai species and their seedlings at between 1 and 5 years after sprouting.

Zelkova seedlings that sprouted about 45 days after a spring planting.

Remove, as you see fit, seedlings that show poor growth.

REPLANTING SEEDLINGS

STEP 1. Be sure to cut the taproot with well-sharpened shears.

STEP 2. Replant the trimmed seedlings in a shallow pot, spreading the roots in all directions.

1. Japanese beech (*Fagus crenata*), first year.

2. Fuji beech (*Fagus crenata*), fourth year.

Japanese beech seeds.

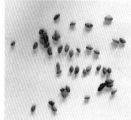

3. Spruce (*Picea*), first year.

Spruce seeds.

4. Japanese black pine (*Pinus thunbergii*), first year.

Japanese black pine seeds.

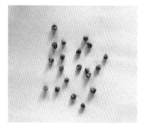

5. Zelkova (*Zelkova serrata*), first year.

Zelkova seeds.

6. Japanese maple (*Acer palmatum*), third year.

Japanese maple seeds.

7. Wax tree (*Rhus succedanea*), first year.

Wax tree seeds.

8. Japanese white pine (*Pinus parviflora*), fourth year (left) and second year.

Japanese white pine seeds.

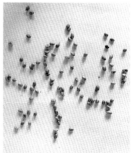

9. Trident maple (*Acer buergerianum*), fifth year.

Trident maple seeds.

10. Oriental bittersweet (*Celastrus orbiculatus*), fifth year.

Oriental bittersweet seeds.

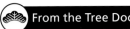

Beginning with this section, occasional comments pertaining to the topic under discussion will be given from the perspective of Masakuni III, a certified a tree doctor.*

There are two seasons suitable for planting seeds. In fall, seeds are sown in mid-fall or later, while for spring planting the seeds are sown after the weather begins to warm. In either case, the condition of the seeds during the preceding winter is key to successful sprouting. The winter cold is essential for germination, and many of the seeds will refuse to sprout in the warmth of spring if they have not been exposed to low temperatures for a long enough time. This is especially true for trees that are native to cold regions.

When preserving seeds over the winter to plant in spring, avoid heated rooms. Rather, keep them in an environment that is similar to their natural outdoor climate, in an area that is not too dry. Do not put the seeds in sealed containers, as they are living, breathing things. Watch out for freezing and overdrying when storing them in a refrigerator. As long as you remember these tips and take proper care during the winter, it is easier and safer to plant the seeds in the spring, when they germinate more quickly than in the fall.

There is one important point to keep in mind when rearing bonsai from seed, namely, that a seed will not always produce a plant with the same qualities as the parent. Most species of trees rarely ever reproduce from one generation to the next purely by virtue of self-pollination. More often, fertilization occurs when pollen from another tree is brought by the wind or insects. So, recalling Mendel's law of heredity, we know that although a tree may have outstanding qualities that make it ideal for a bonsai, a sapling grown from its seed may not inherit all the desired traits. And even if the seed happened to be a product of self-pollination, there is no knowing what unexpected traits it may carry in its genes, for it is impossible to trace the process of pollination by which the parent tree or its ancestors were born.

This factor of genetic variability is not all bad, however. It also holds the potential to yield a plant with entirely new traits that eclipse those of its predecessors. In fact, therein lies the true fun and excitement of starting bonsai from seed. Seeding is believing!

Over the past years, researchers around the world have been decoding and mapping the genomes of living organisms at an enormous pace. The day may not be far off when superior bonsai material will be easily obtainable by scientific methods.

---

* Tree doctors (*jumokui*) in Japan are officially certified experts who have passed an examination accredited by the Ministry of Agriculture, Forestry, and Fisheries of Japan. This ensures that they possess comprehensive knowledge and skills regarding the maintenance, treatment, and recovery of trees based on the physiology, morphology, and pathology of plants, as well as on other scientific disciplines. While the primary role of tree doctors is to regulate the growth of centuries-old trees that are treasured nationally or locally, treat their afflictions, and increase their vigor, they are also more broadly involved in the conservation and cultivation of trees in general. In 1998, Masakuni III became the first bonsai practitioner to receive this certification. There are about a thousand tree doctors in Japan today, but the number of certified tree doctors in the bonsai world remains small.

From the Tree Doctor | Adopting Natural Seedlings

The small maples in the photograph are first-year seedlings that sprouted spontaneously in the spring of the previous year. Their seeds happened to have fallen from a maple tree in my garden into the bonsai pot, where they germinated.

A spontaneously grown plant is perfect for starting a *misho* bonsai, as it is an extremely hardy specimen that has been naturally selected from among numerous seeds. My father has raised many bonsai from maple, zelkova, nettle, and other seedlings that have sprouted spontaneously in pots or my garden by replanting them in individual pots during the repotting season.

Trees drop a large number of seeds every year. Occasionally, seeds are also brought from distant places in the feces of migrating birds. If you look in your immediate surroundings, you are sure to discover fine *misho* seedlings.

Japanese maple seedlings grew from seeds that had fallen into the pot from a garden tree, and are easily repotted for bonsai.

Superfluous branches of Japanese apricot planted in a pot.

Pruned branches planted in the same pot as their source trees.

Recutting the stems in water will keep the ends from coming in contact with the air.

GROWING CUTTINGS

Sashiki

Growing Cuttings

Cuttings of most species can be cultivated, though some are not suitable. The benefit of the cutting, or *sashiki*, method is that you can thereby obtain a plant with exactly the same properties as those of the parent. If there is a tree that has traits desirable in bonsai—the ramification, for instance, or the properties of the leaves or flowers—a clone with identical traits can be made by growing its cutting.

Superfluous branches pruned at the time of repotting or after the tree has come fully into leaf will take root very easily when planted. The cuttings can then be used to start new bonsai. This method also comes in handy when you want to make spares of a precious species in case the original plant dies.

Cuttings are planted either in a fresh pot of fine soil or in the same pot as the source tree. The latter will result in amazingly strong rooting, as the pruned stems are put back in their former environment. Not all types of trees will take root easily by this method. But considering that these are stems that would otherwise go to waste, you might as well try growing them every year, knowing that you will not have lost anything if you fail.

TIPS FOR GROWING CUTTINGS

Here I use the camellia (*Camellia Japonica*) as an example to illustrate the key points for cultivating cuttings.

The stem to be used for *sashiki* must be cut with a very sharp instrument, either at right angles or diagonally. Using a blunt instrument will seriously deform and damage the tissue around the cut, diminishing the likelihood of rooting.

Once the stem is cut, immediately immerse the cut end in water to keep it from drying out and minimize its exposure to air. Recutting it under water is effective, too. Although not commonly done with *sashiki*, this prevents any air from entering the stem and makes it easier for the cutting to draw up water.

Leafy cuttings should be pruned down to just two or three leaves. If you soak the cut end in water overnight and apply rooting hormone to it before planting it,

STEP 1. These cuttings have just two to three leaves left on them. Keep the cut end submerged to prevent exposure to air.

STEP 2. Applying rooting hormone will improve the ability of the cuttings to grow roots.

STEP 3. Insert each cutting into the soil with the end held between the tips of your tweezers so as to protect it during insertion. Once the cutting is in place, remove the tweezers and press down the soil around it to hold it in place.

the cutting will be all the more likely to take root. This way, you can substantially improve the chance of survival with species that are generally said to be unsuitable for growing from cuttings, such as species of pine and maple, by taking care to perform the procedure in the ideal species-specific season (see "From the Tree Doctor," below).

 From the Tree Doctor | ## About Growing Cuttings

In the absence of roots, cuttings absorb water directly. Too many leaves may demand too much water, and there might not be enough to go around. If all the leaves are removed, on the other hand, the cuttings will not be able to draw water effectively. Nor will they be able to photosynthesize and produce the energy they need to grow roots.

Just how many leaves should stay is determined by weighing multiple factors, such as the size of the leaves, the timing of the cutting, the amount of water being fed, and the type of soil. But two or three leaves should be a reasonable esti-

mate, as cuttings are usually made by snipping 2 to 2 1/3 inch (5 to 6 cm) lengths off the ends of young branches.

In general, cuttings of evergreen trees are best taken and planted between late spring and early summer. The ideal season for deciduous trees is in early spring before they bud, which marks the end of the dormant period. Meanwhile, the cuttings of some species that easily take root, such as the ginkgo and oleaster, are not hard to grow even in the height of summer as long as they are watered appropriately.

One technique, which increases the likelihood that cuttings

CUTTING AND STORING

STEP 1. First, an ample length of the branch from which the cutting will be taken is severed from the parent tree. Recut the cuttings in water to between 12 and 16 inches (30 and 40 cm). Shown here are one-year-old branches of zelkova taken from a garden tree. (After using shears in water, thoroughly wipe off the water and apply oil.)

STEP 2. Cover the ends of the cuttings with well-dampened sphagnum moss.

STEP 3. Pull a plastic bag over the moss and tie it with string.

STEP 4. Cover the rest of the cuttings with moistened moss as well.

STEP 5. Roll plastic around the entire length of the moss-covered cuttings. (Air will be able to reach the cuttings, as the plastic is simply wound around them, leaving both ends open.)

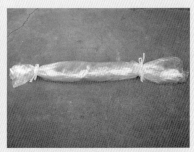

STEP 6. Tie the ends with string. Store the bundle in the refrigerator at a low temperature (41 to 50 degrees Fahrenheit, or 5 to 10 degrees Celsius) until the warmth of spring arrives.

of deciduous trees will take root, requires that one wait until the warm spring season arrives.

The procedure, detailed in six steps on the facing page, should be performed between the end of winter, when the winter buds have adequately swelled, and before the buds open. A cutting is harvested, carefully wrapped, then refrigerated. In the spring the stem is taken out of the refrigerator, and its tip is cut off and planted in soil.

This method effectively exploits the biological cycle of trees. In order to prepare for spring budding, deciduous trees pass the winter with plenty of energy stored within their limbs from the previous spring through fall. The stem is harvested at the peak of its energy level and preserved in that state until it is suitably warm. Then, when the cutting is thrust into the soil, it takes root with surprising speed and opens its winter buds quickly in a rush to catch up with the season. This method thus maximizes the potential for success. It eliminates concerns about unseasonable cold snaps or late frost, and it can also be applied when obtaining bonsai material far from home.

Toriki
Layering

Layering is a convenient way of procuring a desired tree of the desired size. Among the miniature bonsai sold today, those that have been made by layering are quite commonly seen alongside seed-grown plants. Medium-size bonsai can be made by this method as well. In Chapter 4, I outline a layering procedure by which anyone can easily start a bonsai.

Tsugiki
Grafting

There are two great advantages to *tsugiki*, or grafting. The first is that, as with cuttings, it allows you to propagate trees of the same species in large quantities. The second is that by grafting a branch to a fast-growing tree, it will take on the properties of the host plant and develop quite quickly. The method can be used when the source tree is of a highly peculiar species or a rare species with fine qualities for a bonsai, but does not respond very well to cutting. It is also a good shortcut to obtaining future bonsai with mature roots.

The steps for grafting are covered in Chapter 5.

 From the Tree Doctor | **About Grafting**

The stock tree (host) can be chosen not only from the same species as that of the scion (the part that is joined to the host plant) but also from the same genus. For instance, a scion of a red pine (*Pinus densiflora*) can be grafted to a stock of Japanese black pine (*Pinus thunbergii*), both being of the genus *Pinus*. Whereas the success of *sashiki* is determined by the rooting ability of the cutting, a *tsugiki* procedure will have succeeded if the cambium of the scion fuses with that of the stock, and a connection develops between their respective vessels, which convey water from the roots, and their sieve tubes, which conduct sugars from the leaves.

When performing the procedure, sharp tools must be used so as not to damage the cambium tissue.

Yamadori

Collecting Wild Seedlings

While climbing a mountain or hiking, it is not unusual to see young wild-grown saplings or older, stunted trees that have survived many seasons of winter and snow. Digging out such plants and making them into bonsai is called *yamadori*.

A young seedling that does not yet have widespread roots can be harvested immediately, as it will hardly need to have its roots trimmed when potting. It is best to dig up and pot the plant in the appropriate season for repotting that species.

Meanwhile, a tree that has been growing in the wild for several years will usually have developed an extensive root system. You will, therefore, need to prepare the tree in spring and wait at least six months or a year before collecting it. The procedure for preparation is as follows.

Cut the roots all around the periphery of the tree—at a distance equivalent to three to five times the diameter of the tree trunk—as well as underneath it, at a depth equivalent to 1.5 to 2.5 times the trunk's diameter. Replace the tree after this has been done. In about six months to a year, many fine rootlets will have grown from the intact roots. Make sure new roots have sufficiently developed before digging out the plant. Deciduous trees are best collected just before the buds start to open, and conifers and other evergreens should be collected one or two months later. In short, the ideal season for digging up trees is the same as that for repotting them.

If the tree you want to train into a bonsai grows at a high altitude, I recommend that you nurse it at a location halfway down the mountain for about a year, if possible. This will allow the plant to adjust gradually to the change of climate and ensure a greater chance of survival.

Buying at Bonsai Nurseries and Garden Stores

A growing number of bonsai nurseries are opening around the world, and it has become much easier to buy bonsai plants outside Japan. You should have no difficulty finding a plant to your liking, be it a fully mature bonsai, an affordably priced *misho* seedling, or a field-grown plant. To conclude this chapter, I list the main points to note when purchasing a bonsai plant, to ensure finding one that has the potential to become a good bonsai.

Good surface roots

Nebari, or the surface roots (more specifically, the continuity from the flaring trunk base to the spreading surface roots), are of paramount importance. A plant with good *nebari* is sure to make an excellent bonsai. The best shape is that called *happo nebari*, in which the surface roots radiate evenly in all directions. A plant with lopsided root distribution is best avoided unless such an arrangement serves a specific purpose, such as use in a group planting.

Nebari are one of the most important features of a bonsai. Look for a well-shaped trunk base and surface roots when selecting specimens.

Tapering trunk and branches

The trunk and branches should taper gradually from base to tip. A plant of this shape is described as having good *kokejun*, or taper. It is ideal if the trunk has a contour that pleases you, but this is not essential, as the trunk can be trained into the desired shape.

Wild trees occasionally have cracks or large scars on their trunks. A plant of this kind is worth purchasing if it can be made into a *sabamiki* (split-trunk) bonsai. But if the upper part of the trunk has been cut off, the plant should be avoided unless you are very confident of your skill; it will take a long time and exceptional craftsmanship to turn it into a fine bonsai.

Abundant branches

Buy a sparsely branched tree only if you intend to cultivate it in the *bunjin* (literati) style. Otherwise it is best to choose a plant with plenty of branches, for superfluous branches can be cut off at any time. The branches should not be dead or have dead tips, and the tree should be vigorous and well foliated. Healthy, abundant branches with plentiful leaves are a sure sign of good root condition.

A Japanese white pine (*Pinus parviflora*) with good *nebari* (surface roots) and *kokejun* (taper), as well as plentiful leaves and branches.

The new buds of a Japanese white pine (*Pinus parviflora*).

Part 2

TECHNIQUES
Jumpstarting Your Bonsai

The first three chapters discussed the most basic
matters regarding the cultivation of bonsai, including
ways of obtaining bonsai material. In this section
the focus shifts to lesser-known, hands-on techniques,
sometimes involving the use of specific bonsai tools to
create, arrange, and care for bonsai. Through real examples, I explain how using these techniques and selecting
the appropriate tools will maximize your efficiency, and
indicate what outcomes you can expect over time.

CHAPTER 4
Toriki: Layering

On every bonsai shelf, there is likely to be at least one or two specimens like the following: a tree with branches that are unnecessary to the overall balance but have fine curves or other features that make them too good to discard; a tree that has a beautifully curving trunk and handsome branches, but has defective *nebari* (surface roots); or a tree that has fine branches in the upper reaches but none in the middle. These bonsai can be given renewed life as masterpieces using the *toriki*, or layering, method.

The *toriki* method has a number of advantages over other methods by which to start a bonsai:

- A presentable bonsai can be made in a very short time.

- The chances of achieving ideally radiating surface roots are extremely high.

- Material of the desired height (from miniature to medium size) and desired thickness (½ inch to 4 inches, or 1 to 10 cm, in diameter at the layering point) can be easily obtained.

- A new bonsai can be made not only from bonsai with defects, like those given above, but also by using handsome limbs from ordinary trees growing in the garden or elsewhere.

A miniature bonsai made by layering.

In other words, by using the *toriki* method, you can substantially broaden your possibilities for bonsai cultivation.

While the *toriki* method thus has many advantages, it also comes with several challenges. Until now, layering has ordinarily been performed either by fastening wire around the point at which the plant is to be layered or by stripping the bark around that area with a knife. As simple as these operations may seem, they both require considerable expertise to ensure a high chance of success; the former method is affected by how tightly the wire is fastened, the latter by such variables as how thick the bark is and how easy it is to strip off the cambium, which differ by species. But more importantly, the roots will sprout along a straight line by these conventional layering techniques, tending to make the surface roots and trunk appear disjointed for a long time. Photograph 1 shows the base of the trunk of a zelkova that was propagated by the shaving technique about 10 years ago. Even now the traces of the operation are obvious, and there is no

1. The base of a zelkova (*Zelkova serrata*) about 10 years after propagation by layering. This is a typical example of a poorly rooted *toriki* specimen, though the poor state is also due to the roots not having been properly trimmed when the plant was repotted. Specimens like this make perfect material for trying out new *toriki* procedures.

2. The base of a zelkova about 5 years after propagation using a new *toriki* scraper. The surface roots are already taking on a natural appearance.

telling how many more years will have elapsed before the tree looks whole and natural.

Today, however, it has become possible to largely overcome these problems by using a new *toriki* scraper. Photograph 2 shows the base of a zelkova 5 years after it was layered with the *toriki* scraper. The transition from the trunk base to the surface roots appears quite natural, and many people probably would not realize that the *toriki* method had been used unless they were told. The following section explains this method.

A New *Toriki* Method

Most species can be propagated by layering. Here I have selected the internationally popular Japanese maple as an example to illustrate the *toriki* procedure, which is performed in three stages.

STAGE 1

STEP 1. The tree to be used is a Japanese maple (*Acer palmatum*) sapling that sprouted in my garden 10 years ago, now grown to a circumference of about 1 ½ inches (4 cm). The trunk is straight but completely devoid of lower branches, while some of the upper branches are curiously shaped. I will take the upper portion of the tree and make it into a bonsai with well-shaped branches.

STEP 2. Although the branches are few in number, some are unnecessary. These are removed at the base with a spherical knob cutter so as to gouge out part of the stem on which they grow.

STEP 3. The cut should be concave. This is because with some trees, such as maples, the wounds tend to significantly bulge as they heal.

STEP 4. Wound sealant is applied to the wound to prevent infection as well as cracking due to dryness. Select a high-quality sealant that adheres well to the wound. Make sure to apply the sealant thinly and evenly so that no areas of the wound are left uncoated.

The new *toriki* scraper is used here. The bark around the section along the trunk where the roots are to be grown is scraped down to the wood at a width roughly 1.5 times the trunk's diameter at a selected point. It is important to completely strip off both the bark and the cambium all around the circumference.

STAGE 2

STEP 1. The new *toriki* scraper.

STEP 2. To use the *toriki* scraper, lightly apply the blade to the area on which you wish to operate and simply slide it back and forth.

STEP 3. Remove the surface tissue down to the wood.

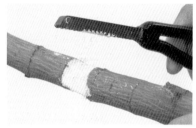

STEP 4. Completely remove the bark around the entire section at a width about 1.5 times its diameter. Without your having to make a special effort, the edges of the stripped area will be more ragged than if a wire or knife had been used, resulting in more natural-looking surface roots.

STEP 5. Be sure to clean the blade after you have finished. Bits of bark between the teeth will stick stubbornly once they have dried, so they should be removed with a brush immediately after use.

STAGE 3

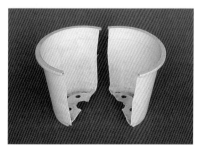

STEP 1. Two halves of a plastic pot are filled with sphagnum moss. The layered bonsai is inserted, and the pot and plant are secured around the layered area with string. Although a plastic bag is an acceptable alternative, I recommend using a plastic pot. A pot is easier to handle, and it has advantages with regard to watering, ventilation, and drainage after the covering has been applied.

STEP 2. Eventually new buds will open. You will know that new roots have sufficiently developed when the young leaves have grown out and hardened.

STEP 3. Look inside the plastic pot and check that new roots have developed adequately.

STEP 4. Saw off the part to be used for the new bonsai at a point somewhat below where the roots have grown. Remove the sphagnum moss and carefully spread out the young roots so as not to damage them. With a root cutter, trim the base to a point just below the roots.

STEP 5. Plant the future bonsai in a training pot. A plant that has been obtained by layering has many young roots developing in all directions and will grow vigorously, so it will need to be repotted the following spring in a display pot and the unnecessary roots will have to be trimmed at the same time.

This concludes the new *toriki* procedure. Its success hinges most of all on whether the flow of substances above and below the operation point has been cut by thoroughly removing a certain width of bark and cambium down to the wood. The chances of root development will be slim if any cambium tissue is left intact so that the upper and lower parts of the plant are still linked. But the new *toriki* scraper takes the hassle out of the procedure and makes it easy for anyone; you need only go around the circumference of the trunk gently scraping the blade back and forth across the surface until the wood is completely bare.

In addition to the ease and certainty of the procedure, the new scraper offers another advantage: the exposed area will not have straight, clear-cut edges as when a wire or knife has been used to pare away the bark, so the roots will grow less artificially. This makes it possible to produce a bonsai with an excellent trunk base and surface roots within a short period.

Layering a tree in the garden.

Using a well-proportioned part of a garden tree for layering.

CHAPTER 5
Tsugiki: Grafting

Tsugiki, or grafting, is highly effective in propagating trees (or parts of trees, such as branches) that possess the same qualities—the properties of the flowers or leaves, for instance—as those of the parent tree. It is used with species that are hard to replicate by *sashiki* (growing cuttings), as well as with many flowering bonsai, such as the Japanese apricot and camellia. The method makes use of a host tree that is already somewhat mature and has mature roots, so it requires much less time to yield a full-grown bonsai compared with growing cuttings that must develop their own roots. And whereas flowering and fruit bonsai cultivated from seed or from cuttings will take years before they begin to bear fruit or flower, grafting offers a shortcut.

The host tree is called the stock, and the branch that is joined to the stock is called the scion. The procedure will succeed only if the cambiums of the stock and scion are joined together so that there is no space between them. The key to achieving this is a sturdy, well-sharpened, single-faced blade. I have seen cheap utility knives with replaceable blades being used, but it is difficult to create flat surfaces with thin, flimsy blades that easily bend or break when used with force. The double-faced blades typical of knives of this type also render them unsuitable for making flat surfaces, the procedure for which requires precision; single-faced blades should be used instead for precision work.

Before using the grafting knife, thoroughly sharpen it on a good, fine-grained whetstone. Being used here is a diamond whetstone, and at right is a traditional Japanese natural finishing whetstone.

As grafting knives are single-faced, with a flat back, both right-handed (left) and left-handed types are available. Like Japanese swords, grafting knives combine hard steel and soft iron. Their edges become extremely sharp when thoroughly honed.

The sharpness of the blade is critical to grafting—in fact, it is the most important factor in determining the success of the procedure. Before use, thoroughly sharpen the grafting knife with a fine-grained whetstone of good quality. Doing so not only enables you to reliably produce angles and flat surfaces but also—importantly—helps minimize the damage to the cellular tissue, leading to swift and healthy fusion of the cambiums.

For best results, perform *tsugiki* on deciduous trees between the end of winter and early spring, and on evergreens in late spring, as the summer heat approaches.

The scion can be grafted onto the stock in several ways, the primary ones of which I explain below.

In *mototsugi* (side grafting), the scion is inserted at the side near the base of the stock. Given readily available stock trees, you can mass-produce material from which to grow bonsai. Side grafting is the most popular grafting method and is used for flowering trees like the camellia and Japanese apricot, for trees of the pine family, and so forth. Japanese black pine trees, known for their distinctive trunks, are propagated by this method.

Grafting the scion onto the top of the stock is called *tentsugi* (top grafting). This method allows you to take advantage of not just the roots of the stock but also the curvature of its trunk, and you can make a bonsai with superlative leaves in a short period. Top grafting is ideal when you want to give an aged appearance to a bonsai of a slow-growing species, such as the Ezo spruce or sargent juniper.

Yobitsugi (approach grafting) is a method of grafting a trunk or branch to a stock without severing the scion from its source. With the source plant still rooted, the area of the scion to be grafted is pulled toward the stock. As well as joining two separate trees, approach grafting can be performed by grafting a branch to another part of the same tree. It is an efficient way of obtaining a well-developed branch where there was no branch to begin with.

When the trunk or a branch has a gap you want to fill, *edatsugi* (branch grafting) can be used to add a branch there. The technique is useful for shaping bonsai of species in which leaves are lacking in the middle sections of the branch, and for altering old bonsai.

I have taken side grafting as an example to demonstrate the *tsugiki* procedure.

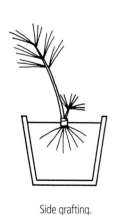

Side grafting.

Top grafting.

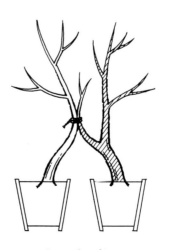

Approach grafting.

Approach grafting.

GRAFTING

STEP **1.** These stocks of Japanese apricot (*Prunus mume*) are about 2 ¾–3 ¼ inches (7–8 cm) tall.

STEP **2.** The scions.

STEP **3.** Hold the stock and knife as shown when cutting into the stock.

STEP **4.** Make an incision in the stock of about the depth shown here. Be sure to leave a thin strip attached.

STEP **5.** The cut.

STEP **6.** Cut off the end of the scion at an acute angle.

STEP **7.** Make another acute-angled cut on the opposite side.

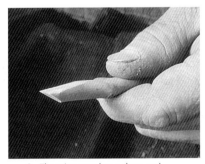

STEP **8.** The scion now has a sharp end.

STEP **9.** Insert the scion into the cut in the stock.

STEP **10.** The joint.

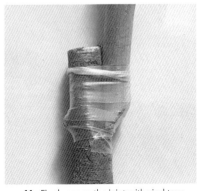

STEP **11.** Firmly secure the joint with vinyl tape.

STEP **12.** Grafting is now complete. Plant the stock in either a pot or a bed of soil.

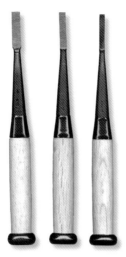

Grafting chisels for branch grafting and other grafting techniques have extremely thin blades that allow you to cut into branches or trunks at the desired angle. From left, the blade widths are $5/16$ inch (7.5 mm), $1/4$ inch (6.0 mm), and $3/16$ inch (4.5 mm).

From the Tree Doctor | Applications of Grafting

Grafting is a magical technique that has vast possibilities beyond simply making clones. Shown here is an example in which a magnificent sargent juniper bonsai is created by making use of approach grafting. The branches in this example are being grafted not just to appreciate them as they are, but to utilize them strategically for various purposes: some will be crafted into *jin* some time after they have taken to the tree, some will be used to help fatten the *mizusui* (lifelines) of the stock, and so forth. Thus, scions are included that are not of the same variety as the stock, in order that the stock may be enriched in a short period.

By grasping the biology and growth of trees and making the various *tsugiki* techniques your own, you may well be able to create impressive bonsai such as this sargent juniper that features dynamic *sharikan* (bone-white deadwood on the trunk) and high-quality leaves.

A masterful sargent juniper (*Juniperus chinensis*) bonsai from multiple grafts.

An example of approach grafting. A smaller plant is grafted to a larger tree and bound (center left), while the pot that contains the smaller tree is secured on the right. Both photographs were taken at Takeo Kawabe's nursery.

CHAPTER 6

Making Bonsai with Multiple Trunks

There are numerous styles of bonsai that have more than one trunk rising up from the roots and are variously called double-trunk, triple-trunk, five-trunk, seven-trunk, or multiple-trunk bonsai, according to the number of trunks. Below I introduce two ways in which you can make bonsai in these styles. Both are very simple and should be easy enough for anyone to try.

Clustering: Growing Plural-Trunk Bonsai with Maple

Trees of the genus *Acer* have a particularly strong tendency to fuse when two trunks are in contact with one another. If you wish to make a multiple-trunk bonsai with one of

Making a plural trunk with maples by clustering.

The same tree 5 years after planting.

The same tree 10 years after planting.

The base of the trunks at 10 years.

The trunks at 20 years.

these species, therefore, there is no need to expose the cambiums and graft the trunks together. By simply planting a desired number of trees of different heights and thicknesses so that their bases are clustered close together, in a few years' time you will have a multiple-trunk bonsai with the trunks naturally merged into one, a technique known as *tsukami-yose*.

The bases of the plants need not be tied together. In fact, tying will only do them harm, because the strings will bite into the trunks as they grow larger. No special tools are used in this technique, but it is essential that you spread the roots carefully at the time of planting, making sure that they do not become entangled, so that the roots can develop in a well-balanced manner.

As with any other style of bonsai, planting is followed by the usual care procedures, from bud trimming and pruning to feeding and repotting. Bonsai with up to about seven trunks can be easily made using this method.

Trunk Cutting: Growing Multiple-Trunk Bonsai

Trees that sprout vigorously, such as the zelkova (*Zelkova serrata*), can be made into multiple-trunk bonsai by growing many shoots from near the base, a process known as *kabudachi*.

The trunk is cut horizontally near the base before the spring sprouting season (step 1). Depending on the size of the trunk, you may use either a saw or a root cutter, the latter of which is capable of cutting thick branches and slim trunks. After the trunk has been cut, give a smooth finish to the whole surface—including the bark—with a sharp graver or knife. Finally, be sure to apply wound sealant on the surface (step 2). This will protect the wound from dry cracking and rotting and will promote the growth of new shoots.

Come the sprouting season, many young shoots will spring forth from around the cut. Based on the number and spacing of trunks you desire, thin out those shoots that are clearly unnecessary. I advise you to leave some extra shoots rather than to immediately reduce them to the desired number, since maybe not all of them will develop into trunks. Shoots that have grown to a certain size should be cut with a concave branch cutter, as it will not be possible to completely remove their base with ordinary trimming shears.

Hereafter, the plant is cared for in the same manner as other bonsai, except that it is usually not defoliated for several years until the trunks and branches are sufficiently thickened. Trim the buds regularly during this period, envisioning the multiple-trunk bonsai in its completed form as you do so.

In addition to the zelkova, the trunk-cutting technique can be used with many other deciduous trees if it is performed at the right time of year. The key is to take to the task with patience after sprouting, giving only as much fertilizer as needed. If you overfeed the plant in a bid to fatten it quickly, balanced growth will be difficult to attain. The most effective path to favorable shoot growth in spring lies in the preparations of the year before: the plant to be made into a multiple-trunk bonsai should be given plenty of vigor by appropriate feeding coupled with adequate water and sunlight.

STEP 1. Tree with cut a trunk to allow new shoots to sprout.

STEP 2. Applying wound sealant.

A zelkova 5 years after the trunk has been cut.

The base and surface roots at 10 years.

CHAPTER 7

Pruning: In Preparation for Repotting

Pruning is a necessary procedure not only when first potting a new bonsai but also before a plant is taken out of a pot for repotting. Bonsai-to-be that have not yet been potted will have unwanted branches that should be removed. Even if you have been taking good care of the plant, there are bound to be branches that have grown too long or are not required. Examples of *imieda* (undesirable branches), which are best pruned before potting, include young shoots that grow pointing up or down from the middle of a horizontal branch, branches that overlap, and branches that grow in threes or more from a single spot. When potting or repotting, it will be easier to determine the placing and the front of the plant if most such branches have been pruned.

TYPICAL EXAMPLES OF UNDESIRABLE BRANCHES

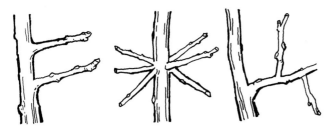

Parallel Branches   Wheel Branches   Upright or Drooping Branches

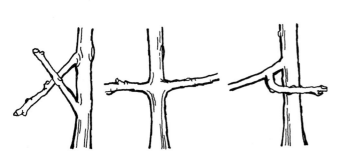

Overlapping Branches   Symmetrical Branches   Trunk-Crossing Branches

Parallel Branches
When two branches grow parallel on one side, cut one of them off.

Wheel Branches
These branches usually grow on azaleas and pine trees. They sprout in all directions from one spot on the trunk. Cut away unnecessary branches.

Upright or Drooping Dranches
Most upright branches are separate shoots and should be cut off whenever they appear. Otherwise, the section from the base of the new shoot to the tip of the old branch will weaken and wither. Downward-growing branches also must be pruned. They interfere with the exposure to sunshine and ventilation of the other branches.

Overlapping Branches
Branches that overlap spoil the shape of the tree; one of them has to be cut off, bent, or separated from the other.

Symmetrical Branches
If two branches grow from one spot and fork to the left and right, one of them is usually cut off. In the case of an upright bonsai, cut off either branch. In the case of a curved bonsai, cut off the branch that is inside the curve.

Trunk-crossing Branches
Branches that cut straight across the trunk are unsightly and should be cut off.

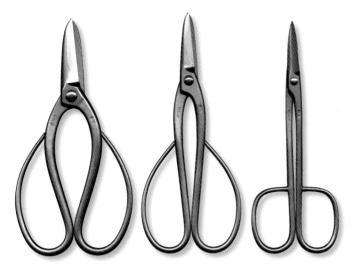

Bonsai trimming shears. These are the most basic bonsai shears, used in a wide variety of situations. From left: general-purpose shears that can easily cut branches with diameters of up to about ¹⁄₂ inch (10 mm); long-shank shears with wide applications that can be used for branches of up to about ¹⁄₄ inch (6 mm) in diameter; shears for thin branches and narrow spaces that can be used for branches of up to about ¹⁄₆ inch (4 mm) in diameter.

It is important to select the shears that best suit the task at hand according to factors such as the diameter of the branch or where you are cutting. The Japanese saying, "The greater serves for the lesser," does not apply to bonsai tools. Neither does the lesser serve for the greater. Thin branches should be trimmed with shears that have narrow ends designed to allow the most delicate pruning, while thin branches in places that are hard to access are cut using narrow-ended shears with a long shank. If you forcibly insert shears that are not long enough to access the inner reaches, you may stress and break some of the precious outer branches. Thick branches must be pruned with shears that are made especially for that purpose. If a branch or root is too thick to be cut with trimming shears, you can instead use gardening shears, a root cutter, or a pruning saw.

Where three branches create a fork, a concave branch cutter is used to remove one of them. Concave branch cutters are versatile tools that can be used for a number of procedures, including to sever ordinary branches from their base and to trim roots. In fact, they may be thought of as general-purpose cutters, as they are capable of cutting parts of plants that are beyond the ability of ordinary shears.

In many plant species, including maples, the scar may swell outward over time if a branch is cut off flat at the base. Either a concave branch cutter with spherical blades

Using a pruning saw.

Pruning with gardening shears.

Pruning with a root cutter.

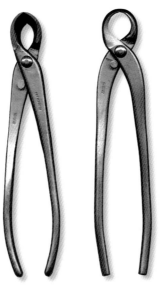

The blades of a spherical-blade concave branch cutter and a spherical knob cutter. Note their rounded shapes.

A concave branch cutter. Concave branch cutters are among the most important bonsai tools and are available in a range of sizes and blade shapes.

A concave branch cutter with a spherical blades (left), and a spherical knob cutter. Both produce concave, spherical cuts.

or a spherical knob cutter is suitable in these instances, since they both create concave cuts. If you cut a branch flat across with ordinary shears, you will then need to carve out the wound with a graver or other tool in order to prevent bulging during the healing period. But by using one of the suggested tools, you will be able to complete both the cutting and the carving in one action. Eventually, the wound will become flat and indistinguishable, as shown in the photographs on page 61.

Concave branch cutters allow you to nicely trim three-pronged branches, which are difficult to cut with ordinary trimming shears. A concave cut heals more cleanly than a flat cut.

With concave branch cutters you can completely sever branches from their base. Note the concave cut.

Imieda, or undesirable branches, are considered aesthetically unnecessary, but at this early stage they are vital since they support the life of the plant. While a tree will never do anything that is nonessential to its subsistence and growth, it will always try to do whatever is needed to survive, without any regard for our human sense of aesthetics. Pruning a branch that we consider unnecessary without careful thought could disrupt the balance of the tree, especially if it is a thick branch that produces many leaves. In order to make up for the loss and regain balance, the tree will become prone to sprouting more "unnecessary" branches that are in fact necessary for its well-being. Thus, beware of cutting branches excessively, and try to predict the possible outcome as you prune branches, so that you can cope appropriately with eventualities.

In some cases it is advisable to postpone the pruning of unnecessary branches, including *imieda*, to aid the growth of the trunk and branches. See the figure for an example. Branch A is clearly an *imieda* and should eventually be pruned. But, as branch B below is frail compared to branch C, you can continue to allow it to draw on the energy produced by photosynthesis in branch A to enhance the growth of branch B. Branch A is cut off after its work has been completed.

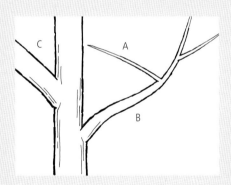

Skillfully utilizing "unnecessary" branches in this way will enable you to achieve a good balance in the thicknesses of the trunk and branches in a short space of time. In contrast with the artificial approach of heavy fertilization, it is a natural approach to bonsai cultivation that better suits the physiology of trees. If you look in the nursery of a skilled cultivator, you will notice that a surprising number of branches that appear unnecessary to the overall shape of the tree are initially left intact.

As effective a technique as it is to wait for a while before cutting off these branches, there is one important fact that must be kept in mind: whereas a thin branch can be thickened, a branch once grown thick cannot be slimmed down.

Though this may seem obvious, it is good to remember this fact, since the optimum period for pruning is limited. Be sure not to miss the right timing to cut off the branches in question, calculating the plant's growth until next spring.

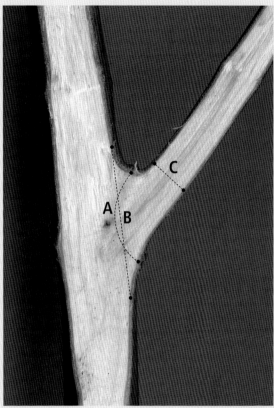

When pruning a branch, cut as in line A to decrease the area of the wound. You would ordinarily want to prune as in line B, but this would create a much larger wound that will take time to heal. Wounds should heal as quickly as possible. If you cut off the branch so as to leave a stub, as in line C, the bark will not be able to grow over the wound.

If you prune a branch incompletely, as in line C, the wound will not be covered by bark, as shown here. With species that decay easily, an uncovered cut will eventually result in a hole in the plant.

Some species, such as the *satsuki* azalea (*Rhododendron indicum*) and several other exceptional plants, must have their branches cut off flat, since the wound tissue will not swell. In such cases, thick branches are pruned with a root cutter made specifically for a flat cut, and thin branches with a knob cutter or a crescent-blade branch cutter, so that the wound is flush with the surface of the trunk.

The pruning tools that have been introduced in this section are available in a range of sizes to handle thick branches, thin branches, and branches in hard-to-reach places.

After you have pruned the plant properly with well-sharpened tools, be sure to treat the wounds. Small wounds as well as large ones take time to heal, so if untreated, they are at risk of such problems as bacterial infection, fissures caused by overdrying, and excessive dieback. To minimize the problems, wound sealant is applied. Coat the wound with a thin, even layer of sealant, taking care that none of it runs over the edge of the wound. A multitude of protective agents are marketed as having this or that benefit, but the critical question is how well the agent adheres to the wound. Moreover, the sealant should peel off naturally as bark develops over the wound, so that it does not hinder bark growth.

PRUNING THICK BRANCHES

STEP **1.** Cut off the branch near the base with a pruning saw, then finish with a series of small cuts using a root cutter.

STEP **2.** Partially trimmed branch.

STEP **3.** To finish, cut off what remains using a root cutter.

STEP **4.** The wound is now flat. Apply wound sealant thinly and evenly to protect the wound. Use this technique for plants with thin skins.

Pruning marks on a trident maple: The marks from three years ago, seen in the upper parts, have mostly healed. The wound sealant that was applied for protection has already fallen off. There also was a large wound in the middle, but it has healed so fully that you must look carefully to find it. Six years have elapsed since the branch was pruned, and the roundness of the wound is hardly noticeable.

Pruning marks on a Japanese maple. Even large pruning wounds will heal as well as those on this tree if the branches have been pruned properly. The mark on the left is from three years ago, and the one at center is from five years ago.

Viewing the same tree from a different angle, you can see that the large pruning mark has become nearly flat.

CHAPTER 8

Repotting

It is a grave warning sign to have bonsai with soil that has risen prominently into a mound. The pot of such a bonsai is crowded with roots—a condition called *nezumari*, or root clogging. It happens when a bonsai has not been repotted for years. Water will not penetrate the soil well, and the soil is very poorly ventilated. If left like this for too long, some of the roots may die from either dehydration or suffocation, potentially inducing not just partial dieback of the branches but the death of the entire plant.

The domed state of the soil indicates that the roots are overcrowded.

Potted bonsai need to be regularly repotted to prevent root clogging and to invigorate the roots. The appropriate interval is somewhere between one and five years depending on the species, the bonsai's age, and the care it is being given, such as defoliation and pruning. Generally speaking, the younger the plant, the more frequently it needs to be repotted. Meanwhile, there also are quite a few trees that need to be repotted every year even after they are mature. But details aside, the basic rule is to keep an eye on your plant and repot it before the roots become cramped.

As repotting is important and necessary, many handbooks instruct readers on the method and procedures. However, most of them discuss age-old and time-consuming methods that are performed with the minimum of tools, and cultivators have always sought ways to accelerate the procedures.

Repotting, which ordinarily involves trimming a lot of roots in the open air, puts a heavy strain on the plant. It may be compared in human terms to an abdominal operation—and a major one at that. To minimize the strain on and damage to the plant, it must be repotted as efficiently as possible by using the appropriate tools and procedures.

Also crucial is the timing. A plant cannot be repotted at just any time; the best season to repot a plant safely and achieve favorable results is highly limited. Basically, any procedure related to the care of bonsai needs to be carried out at the right time, but in no other procedure can the consequences of wrong timing be as disastrous as those of repotting. Untimely repotting could, in the worst case, directly lead to the plant's death. Thus, however many bonsai you have that need to be repotted, you must repot all of them within a limited period. For this reason, it is essential that you be able to perform the procedures swiftly.

Although it has been difficult to reduce the time it takes to repot by conventional methods, a variety of newly developed tools has transformed the related procedures and improved efficiency by a large margin. Those of you who own many bonsai will have a lot of work on your hands during the repotting season. But by using the tools introduced here, you will be able to save precious time, as well as protect the life and health of your bonsai.

By using the repotting sickle and newly developed repotting tools like the double-edged bonsai sword, you should be able to complete the process in about a third of the time it would take by conventional methods.

REPOTTING

STEP 1. Use a repotting sickle if the plant is in a deep pot or a pot with rounded sides, or if you are otherwise having difficulty removing it from the pot. Insert the blade along the edge of the pot and cut around the circumference. A plant in a deep pot can be removed more easily and efficiently after the sickle has been circled around several times, gradually going deeper until it reaches the bottom. The roots filling the rounded part of the pot will be severed along with the soil around them, and the plant can then be lifted out with ease. It will take tremendous time and effort just to unpot the bonsai if you go about loosening the soil around the edge of the pot inch by inch with a stick or similar tool.

STEP 2. To remove a plant from a pot that is deeper than the sickle can reach, use the new double-edged bonsai sword. Insert the blade inside the edge of the pot until it hits the bottom, and cut the neighboring roots by moving it side to side. After the roots in that area have been freed, shift the blade to a new position and cut the roots there. Repeat the process until you have worked your way around the pot.

STEP 3. Lift the plant out of the pot. Without loosening the soil, go around the circumference, cutting back the root ball about one-third of the way in with the bonsai sword.

STEP 4. Cut away about one-third of the roots from the bottom.

STEP 5. Cut away the soil and roots between the thick radiating roots in wedges. Up until this point, the soil clinging to the roots is not loosened.

STEP 6. Finally, loosen the outer roots with a small hand rake or other suitable tool.

STEP 7. With trimming shears, a root cutter, or concave cutter, trim the thick roots that stick out. The plant is now ready to be potted again.

When replanting, select a pot that suits the shape of the plant and the appropriate type of soil, then carefully determine where the front of the pot will be and where exactly in it to place the plant.

Water the plant well as soon as you are done. As it has just been freshly repotted, care must be taken not to wash away the topsoil when watering. Rather, you should sprinkle water on the soil until the water running out of the drainage hole becomes perfectly clear; think of it as rinsing rather than watering the soil. In fact, one of the goals is to rinse the powdered soil particles from the soil as best you can soon after repotting. This is vital for the healthy growth and activity of new roots.

Primary tools used in repotting. Select the tools that suit the size of the bonsai you are repotting. From left: small, medium, and large trowels; repotting sickle; bonsai sword; bonsai sword for deep pots; two-pronged and three-pronged rakes for loosening the roots; rake for miniature bonsai; single-pronged rake; hard and soft hemp-palm brooms; and bamboo chopsticks.

The Importance of Roots

A good bonsai will always have good roots, and good roots will always nurture a good bonsai. The way to grow intricate branches on bonsai of deciduous trees is to encourage the even growth of rootlets by cutting back uneven, excessively thick roots when repotting. The shape of the tree can be altered or modified at any time, but its roots can be adjusted only when it is being repotted. In effect, repotting is the sole chance to work on creating well-proportioned radial roots. Be sure to understand the importance of roots in bonsai cultivation and make good use of the opportunity presented by repotting. Since the new repotting tools allow you to save a lot of time, you should be able to devote plenty of time to observing and trimming the roots.

The base and surface roots of a zelkova at 20 years from seed.

THE ROOTS OF WILD TREES

With very few exceptions, large trees standing strong against wind and rain have surface roots distributed almost perfectly in all directions. Moreover, these roots slope down into

This bonsai, a Chinese hackberry, exudes a natural elegance due to its well-balanced root structure.

the earth at an angle of 30 degrees or less—most frequently around 15 degrees—relative to the surface. The angle formed naturally by these roots shows the optimal resistance to external forces like high winds, and we cannot help but marvel at the great wisdom of nature. Incidentally, the sleepers of railroad rails are also laid at an angle of 15 degrees. The strength provided by this angle against horizontal forces has been scientifically proven.

By growing surface roots at this angle, you will be able to create a bonsai that expresses the grandeur of a giant tree. The Chinese hackberry seen here is one such example. The surface roots slope down at a 15-degree angle and beautifully radiate from the trunk in every direction.

Below, for your reference, I give you basic instructions on how to create the kind of surface roots described above.

step 1. Plant the tree in a shallow pot; do not use a deep pot. The depth ideally should be no more than the diameter of the trunk at its base.

step 2. Cut off the roots growing directly under the trunk and repot the tree with the roots distributed evenly.

step 3. Each time you repot the tree, use a root cutter to remove from its base all the roots extending down.

From the Tree Doctor | When to Repot

No definite time frames for repotting can be given on a single universal calendar. This is because the progression of temperatures in spring widely varies from region to region, and also because the environment affects how soon the trees become active. Instead, several guidelines are offered below to help you decide when to repot your deciduous bonsai. The optimum season in your region is when:

- The trees are not leafed.
- There is minimal need to cut back freshly grown roots.
- The wounds from pruning or trimming are able to heal relatively swiftly.

When applied to Tokyo, Japan, which is situated in the temperate zone, the guidelines suggest that the best time for repotting is between early February and early March; that is, at the end of winter and the cusp of spring. This happens to coincide with the Kokufu Bonsai Exhibition held every year in Tokyo. Since temperatures begin to rise from around this time as the days lengthen, the trees will immediately spring to life.

Trimming the branches at the same time is also a good idea. As trees promptly become active in early spring, they will be able to recover quickly.

Repotting should be done before new roots begin to develop. In the case of early sprouters like the Japanese maple, with roots that become active equally early, many experts recommend repotting in late fall after the tree has defoliated. If you do so, though, and depending on where you live, you may need to take precautions to protect your plant from the winter cold by, say, keeping it indoors.

As for pines and other evergreens, the optimum season for repotting is generally a little later than the season for deciduous trees. In the Tokyo area, for example, evergreens are said to be best repotted around the time that deciduous trees come into full leaf—after the cherry blossoms have fallen and the weather has become warmer. You can deduce the right time to repot your evergreen bonsai by referring to common flowers and deciduous trees in your region.

When the buds are about to open and the trees are in a high-energy state is the perfect time to safely repot Japanese white pines.

By following these directions, you should be able to achieve satisfactory results by the third repotting, with no more roots growing under the trunk and the remaining roots spread out evenly.

Use fertilizer somewhat liberally for good results, though overuse should be avoided.

Soil

As a topic related to repotting, I would like to discuss the soil used in bonsai. I use Japanese *akadama* soil for nearly all of my bonsai, but every tree will generally fare best in its native soil, so if you can find suitable soil in your country, that should really be your best bet. (For more information on Japanese soil types, see the Appendix.) Because there is such a profusion of information about the suitability of each soil for various species and about the mixing of different soils, people often seem to have the impression that selecting and using the appropriate type of soil is a complicated affair. But there is no need to complicate the matter—you should nearly always be able to achieve good results if you observe the following points.

This set of five sieves—with mesh sizes of 1/24 inch (1 mm), 1/8 inch (3 mm), 1/5 inch (5 mm), 1/3 inch (7 mm), and 1/2 inch (10 mm)—will enable you to produce bonsai soil of virtually every necessary coarseness.

- Use quality sieves. The first and basic point is to use good sieves with which you can reliably obtain grains of the desired size.

- Remove powdered soil particles of 1/24 inch (1 mm) or less. A sieve should be used to remove tiny particles from the soil, since they undermine both the permeability and the drainage of the soil and potentially kill or rot the roots.

- Use fine soil for fine branches. Fine grains of 1/8 inch (3 mm) or less are used for deciduous species like the Japanese maple and zelkova to achieve good results. Alongside bud trimming and defoliation, using fine-grained soil is one of the major keys to producing delicate branches on deciduous bonsai. Rootlets will develop well, and the tips of the branches will not grow thick but into numerous fine branchlets.

- Allow for good drainage. Spread soil with a large grain size of 1/5 inch (5 mm) or more to about 20 percent of the pot's depth before adding the planting soil. This will improve drainage as well as ventilation at the bottom of the pot, greatly enhancing the health of the roots and therefore of the overall tree.

For still more effective removal of powdered soil particles, you can use meshed sieve scoops to pour the soil into the pot.

- Repot in fresh soil. It is best to repot with fresh soil that has been carefully sieved. Careless reuse of old soil is likely to cause problems with fertilizer residue, bacteria, or weed seeds mixed in the soil. If you do reuse old soil, you must first rinse away all fertilizer residue. This can be done by exposing the soil to the natural cleansing action of rain for about a year, then drying and sterilizing it by spreading it out in a large space and exposing it to plenty of sunlight.

- Soil for miniature bonsai. There is no need to prepare special soil for miniature bonsai; regular bonsai soil will do. But as miniature bonsai are planted in small pots, the grain size generally should be no larger than about 1/8 inch (3 mm).

Powdered soil particles of ¹⁄₂₄ inch (1 mm) or less must be completely removed before the soil is used.

The above are the basic points to remember when using planting soil. On a final note, be sure to check the soil pH level preferred by each species before planting.

 From the Tree Doctor | ## Getting to Know the Soil

It is no exaggeration to say that the soil nurtures your bonsai 24 hours a day, 365 days a year. Watering is the daily practice of every bonsai cultivator, but it is the soil, which is in constant contact with the roots, that supplies water over the longer term. Every day, in a manner of speaking, you are delegating to the soil the task of watering the roots. In other words, the soil controls moisture and, hence, the growth of bonsai.

The first thing you need to know when selecting soil is how much water each soil can hold—its water retentivity. Water retentivity varies by soil type, but it is also considerably affected by grain size. The smaller the grains, the more water the soil can contain, because water is retained in the gaps between the grains by the same principle as capillary action, whereby water rises through a thin tube. The water retained in the soil is in fact called capillary water, and it is this capillary water that the roots absorb. (For those readers who want more detailed information, take a look at the table for Japanese soils in the Appendix that compares the water retentivity of the major types of planting soil. From the soil descriptions, you will usually be able to find the equivalents for your local soil. You should be able to learn a lot by studying the chart, and I encourage you to try measuring the water retentivity of your soils by the same method.)

If the soil accumulates more water than the roots need, this will interfere with root respiration. The soil needs to be able to drain water as well as hold it, so that air can pass through the gaps between the grains and keep the soil well ventilated. From the standpoint of the roots, the soil encasing them is simultaneously clothing, bedding, and housing, and it is your job to maintain a comfortable environment for the roots.

There are two kinds of soil structures: a single-grain structure has loose grains, whereas an aggregate structure comprises individual grains clumped together. Aggregate soil is capable of holding more water than single-grain soil and creates more space between the clumps. This structure is the most important feature that enables the soil to nurture good bonsai. Its benefits will be diminished, however, if the clumps are too small or irregularly sized, or if powdered soil particles get mixed in. This is where sieves, which allow you to unify grain sizes, are so crucial.

In addition to the physical properties, the chemical properties of the soil need to be considered as well. Most tree species will do just fine in soil that is either neutral (pH 7.0) or slightly acidic (around pH 6.5). Although many trees can survive in other environments, it is usually better not to stray outside the given range. I recommend keeping litmus papers or a pH meter on hand so that you can always check the soil's pH level. If it is inappropriate, adding lime can provide a temporary fix. But this trick should be reserved for emergencies due to a feeding error or other slipup, and I would advise against routinely using lime to adjust the pH level.

Any soil from any country can be used if it meets the physical and chemical conditions given above. I see many bonsai books that spell out which soils should be mixed at what ratio for each species, but few go into the details of why and for what purpose the soils must be mixed in a given way or what grain sizes should be used. Some soils are easy to obtain, while others are hard to find. Bonsai of the same species may be found or raised in different conditions, as the climate and environment will vary from place to place. A bonsai may be healthy or weak (recovering from major surgery), young or old, large or small. Furthermore, each cultivator will envision different future shapes for their bonsai. Thus, while it may seem helpful to have the soil mixture ratio for each species, this could in fact be a major reason the selection of soil has impressed bonsai cultivators as a challenging affair.

Instead of mixing different soils, you can use just one type of soil, the water retentivity and drainage of which can be changed quite easily by adjusting the mix of the grain size. Raising diverse species in the same soil will teach you a lot about the differences in the growth attributes of each species. I believe it is safest to use simple, unenriched soil that you have properly sieved as your basic planting soil, adding fertilizer only as needed.

Having gained a firm awareness of the role and importance of soil, your first step is to find a readily available soil that satisfies the necessary conditions, and to learn its characteristics through hands-on experience. As you improve your understanding of soil, you should become able to make accurate choices based on the condition of a plant or the future you envision for that plant, as well as utilize the soil in a more strategic manner.

CHAPTER 9

Metsumi: Bud Trimming

Spring is the season in which new buds unfurl. Each tree, however, will bud differently. The amount of sunlight and the temperature greatly affect the manner of budding, as does the health of the individual tree. Bonsai that have been kept well from the year before will bud vigorously, whereas those that have received improper care or repotting will bud poorly. Spring budding is like a report card on the care you have given your bonsai over the previous year.

The young buds that have sprouted should not be left to grow unchecked. In bonsai, bud trimming is always performed, for it is fundamental to determining and maintaining the shape of your bonsai. Bud trimming allows you to control branch length and create intricate branching. If you neglect the task, you may end up with longer branches, which will deform a bonsai that you have already trained into shape. Trimming the buds is particularly vital for achieving intricately ramifying ends that do not crisscross—a major highlight of deciduous bonsai.

As a general rule, the buds of deciduous trees are trimmed by keeping just the first two leaves and nipping off what extends beyond them (though if you want the shoot to grow out, you can wait until it reaches the desired length and trim the end later if it grows any longer); a new bud will emerge from between the remaining leaves. The branches of any bonsai should always bifurcate. Where you can foresee buds growing into trifurcating branches, bud trimming is performed so that just two branches will be left.

Trimming the buds of a Japanese maple. Always use well-sharpened bud-trimming shears and cut off the bud cleanly.

The young buds of deciduous trees are vigorous in early spring, and they will grow out in no time if you neglect to trim them for two or three days. Cultivators who own many deciduous bonsai are thus kept very busy in spring. But the bustle of bud trimming also is part of the zest of bonsai cultivation and is to be enjoyed.

Spring is budding season for pines and other evergreens. With evergreen trees that tend to grow buds in threes—like the Japanese black pine—the large central bud is usually removed. The remaining shoots may be trimmed back from around the middle to adjust the balance in sizes if they grow out too long. Clusters of four or more buds are similarly trimmed down to just two buds and proportionally adjusted.

Many specialists and experts recommend trimming the buds of pines and other conifers with the fingernails instead of shears. There are good reasons for this. The first is that if you use shears and accidentally cut off the tip of a bud you want to keep, the leaves will have unsightly incisions when they unfurl. The second reason is that you should

Trimming the buds of a Japanese black pine. Ordinarily, the central bud is trimmed if there are three buds growing in the same place.

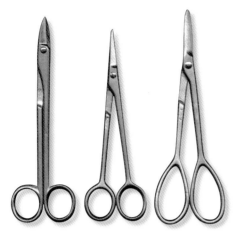

Bud-trimming shears. Be sure to select the appropriate shears for the species and part of the tree on which you are working, as bud trimming is a highly delicate task. From left to right: shears with a long, slender shank for trimming buds in narrow and deep spots; shears for Japanese white pines, with an especially fine tip and an open shank that will not pinch leaves; shears with wide applications that can also be used to prune miniature bonsai.

not miss the right timing—that is, using your fingers means that you must remove the buds while they are tender enough to be easily trimmed with the fingernails.

While both of these points are highly important, the majority of cultivators will find it difficult to accurately aim their fingernails at the point at which they want to trim the buds. There is considerable danger of trimming at the wrong place, scratching the bonsai, or removing from its base a bud that you intended to keep. The risk is even greater with trees for which rebudding is a delicate matter, like the Japanese white pine, or if you are trimming the buds rather late. In the light of the delicacy of the procedure, therefore, correctly using bud-trimming shears is the safest and surest option for the general cultivator, even given a full understanding of the points noted above.

The paramount requirements for bud-trimming shears are high-precision blades capable of cutting at exact locations and sufficient sharpness to keep the shears from damaging the surrounding tissue. In addition, the shape of the shank must be carefully designed so as not to stress or pinch the neighboring branches and leaves.

With some species and parts of bonsai, it can also be highly effective to use a branch cutter with fine tips that are capable of completely removing buds from their base.

When trimming the buds of trees like the Japanese white pine, use shears that have an open shank, so that you do not pinch any leaves between the handles.

Use shears with a long, slender shank to accurately trim the buds on *yoseue* (group planting) and bonsai with closely growing branches, as well as buds located in deep parts of a bonsai.

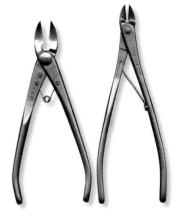

The crescent-blade branch cutter (left) and twig cutter. These special branch cutters, with their narrow blades, are used for trimming the buds of plants like the azalea. They are capable of completely removing from their base new buds and twigs in various places.

With narrow blades and shanks of ample length, these branch cutters can remove the azalea's buds, buds in deep places, and twigs, all without leaving a stub.

Hagari: Defoliation

After a period of bud growth, during which you have regularly trimmed the buds of deciduous bonsai, the growth of new buds will cease, and the young leaves will darken and harden. The trees are best defoliated at this time.

You have been trimming buds in order to keep the branches from growing too long, and to produce intricate branches. Removing the leaves encourages further ramification—it prompts the tree to put forth new buds, in effect growing two years' worth of fine branchlets in one year. Thus, defoliation is a highly effective way of creating delicate branches on deciduous bonsai.

Defoliation also miniaturizes the leaves. For this reason, it is ordinarily performed on the entire tree, but you may alternatively cut off just those leaves near the tips of the branches. Although it will be difficult to make the leaves uniformly small by this method, you will be able to achieve intricate ramification without putting a large strain on the tree.

Even if you are defoliating the entire plant, let the leaves remain on branches that are weak. This is to adjust the vigor of the branches. Young leaves that are just beginning to unfurl should be left untouched as well.

I still occasionally see people pinching off the leaves with their fingers, but damaging the tree by this method is a real possibility. You may inadvertently peel off the bark around the base of the leaf, for instance, or you may break a branch while trying to insert your hand in between crowded branches. Hence, it is safer to use defoliating shears.

The leaves of trees like maples are cut off at the middle of the stem. Leaves that have no stem, such as those of the zelkova, are cut off at the base. The remaining stems and bases will eventually fall off.

Defoliating shears are tweezer-shaped shears that are hinged at the rear end so that they can be repeatedly opened and closed with minimal effort. Their slender form makes it possible to reach comfortably into crowded or deep places and manipulate them safely and precisely. Although removing the multitude of leaves requires patience, you can work efficiently by starting at the crown and gradually working down with these shears.

The condition of the branch ends will be clearly visible once you have defoliated the tree. If you find that you have overlooked any buds and unintentionally allowed some branches to grow long, be sure to readjust them at this time using bud-trimming shears.

Subsequently, keep watering the plant from above, with the aim of protecting it from dehydration, until new buds emerge. Watch out for overwatering, however, as the tree's

Defoliating shears.

Defoliating a trident maple. Leaves of the genus *Acer* are removed from the middle of the stem.

The stemless leaves of zelkovas are removed at the base. If you have difficulty removing them from the base, you can cut them off so as to leave part of the base.

ability to draw up water is weak at this time. Water the tree generously once the leaves begin to open, and also give it plenty of sunlight if it is a species that prefers sun. New buds should be regularly trimmed.

If you wish to grow buds on pine trees, such as the Japanese black pine, or if you wish to adjust the dynamic balance between the branches on such trees, you can pluck the needles with pine tweezers that are specially made for this purpose. Carefully pull out each needle in its precise direction of growth, as you may hurt the base of the needle if you pull it in the wrong direction. In the case of needles that are hard to pluck, or if you feel unsure about using tweezers, you can instead use bud-trimming shears with narrow blades to safely cut off the needles somewhat above the base. What remains of the needles will eventually fall off.

With pine trees, grasp the needles one at a time with special pine tweezers and pull them out in their direction of growth.

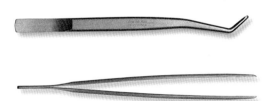

Pine tweezers with angled tips (top) and straight tips.

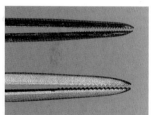

Compare the tips of ordinary tweezers (top) with those of pine tweezers. Pine tweezers have larger and deeper notches with which to securely grasp the needles.

CHAPTER 11
Training and Reshaping

You have read in Chapter 2 that there are many bonsai styles. But plants will not necessarily grow into the desired form of their own accord. You may be able to finely ramify the branches by performing bud trimming and defoliation, but as you work your bonsai toward the shape you envision, you are bound to come up with various modifications that you would like to make. You may want to bend a branch further, for instance, or you may want to change a curve in the trunk. Among the specimens that you have been growing for many years, too, there could be several that will become more attractive if you train the branches or trunk, or if you alter the entire shape. To a greater or lesser extent, most bonsai will need to have their shapes adjusted or altered by such procedures as bending and straightening.

Today an assortment of tools is available for easy bending and straightening in almost any situation. With these tools it is possible to reshape the contour of the trunk—as well as of the branches—at will.

Wiring

Branches are occasionally pulled with rope or wire to lower them or change their direction, but most training procedures consist of wiring—bending or straightening branches and trunks by wrapping them with wire of the correct gauge.

Two types of wire are used in bonsai: aluminum wire and copper wire, most commonly between gauges no. 6 and no. 24. Steel wire is rarely used today, as rust is detrimental to bonsai. When using copper wire, select wire with one-fifth to one-third the diameter of the trunk or branch around which it will be wound, or double the wire if a single strand does not provide enough strength. When using aluminum wire, select wire that is about two gauges heavier than the appropriate copper wire. Whether aluminum or copper, heavy wires are generally hard to wrap around trees and could hurt the bonsai in narrow places. In such instances, it is safer to use multiple strands of wire that are one or two gauges lower.

Always use copper wire that has been annealed. Fully annealed copper wire is highly pliable and easy to manipulate, but it will become very rigid once it has been wrapped. The phenomenon, called "work hardening," occurs with aluminum wire as well, but not to as great a degree. This, in addition to the difference in the strengths of the metals,

WIRING THE TRUNK

STEP 1. Use wire pliers to insert one end of the wire deep into the soil between the roots and anchor it in place.

STEP 2. Wind the wire around the trunk toward the apex at a 45-degree angle.

STEP 3. The spirals of the wire should be more or less equally spaced.

STEP 4. Finish by securing the wire firmly to the tree with wire pliers.

Wrapping wire around a pair of branches.

Small wire pliers with a fine tip come in handy when wiring the ends of the branches.

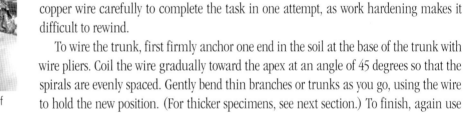

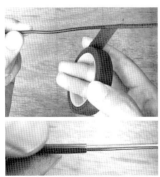

Wrapping wire with a paper tape (top), and covering it with a plastic tube.

is why copper wire is more potent than aluminum wire of the same gauge. Wrap the copper wire carefully to complete the task in one attempt, as work hardening makes it difficult to rewind.

To wire the trunk, first firmly anchor one end in the soil at the base of the trunk with wire pliers. Coil the wire gradually toward the apex at an angle of 45 degrees so that the spirals are evenly spaced. Gently bend thin branches or trunks as you go, using the wire to hold the new position. (For thicker specimens, see next section.) To finish, again use wire pliers to neatly fasten the upper end.

When wiring branches, a single wire is often used to wrap two branches—an upper branch and a lower branch, or a pair of diverging limbs.

Employ thin wires for the ends of the branches. Small wire pliers with fine tips will enable you to work comfortably in narrow places and to fasten the end securely. These small pliers are also used for unwiring.

If the bonsai you are wiring has thin, delicate bark, wrap the wire with paper tape or pull it through a plastic tube to protect the bark.

It is essential that you do not wind the wires too tightly but keep them somewhat loose. Apply wire with the idea of gently embracing the tree with it, not of pulling it tightly around the trunk or branch. Firmly wrapped wire will quickly scar the tree's surface as the tree grows, especially if the wire is aluminum. The difference between aluminum and copper lies in their rates of thermal expansion; the former expands and contracts nearly twice as much as the latter.

The time that will elapse before the tree's growth causes the wires to scar the surface and begin biting into the bark varies by season, the species of tree, and its growing condition. But on average, the wires will bite into the hard bark of, say, a Japanese black pine from about the sixteenth week after wiring, and into the soft bark of maples from around the seventh week.

The role of wiring is analogous to that of a cast that is applied to a broken arm or leg of a human being. When you change the shape of a branch or trunk, you are bruising the cells in that area, and wiring is applied to stabilize and protect it until the cells have healed. The wires will begin biting into the tree when the bruised tissue has completely healed and the branch or trunk—now fixed in its new shape—resumes growth. The wires must be removed at this juncture, or they will scar your bonsai. You can rewire a tree any number of times, but scars that have once formed will remain for many years. Be very careful not to miss the right time to unwire.

Unwiring

Bonsai are meant to be appreciated in their natural, unwired form. Wires should, therefore, be removed as soon as their purpose has been accomplished.

You will be able to efficiently remove thin wires on the tips of branches by using the same small wire pliers that were used in wiring. But there is a great risk of damaging branches and leaves if you try to unwind with your hands or pliers heavier wires that have hardened. In other parts of the tree, therefore, it is best to cut off the wires in short lengths using a wire cutter. This method is easy on the tree, and you will be able to work safely, reliably, and efficiently. Moreover, it will allow you to check how well the bonsai's shape has been corrected even as you remove the wiring.

There are two important precautions that I would like you to remember when working with wire. The first is that wire should always be cut squarely, whether you are applying or removing it, as pointed ends can be very dangerous. Do not leave scraps of wire scattered in or around the pot; immediately clear them away when you are done. The second precaution is to always use a wire cutter that has sufficient strength for the material and gauge of the wire. The cutter could break if you try to sever heavy wire with one that is designed for thin wire, and there is then the further danger of a broken blade or wire flying off. I advise you to conduct the procedure with caution and certainty by correctly using a suitable tool for the task at hand.

This young tree is scarred with wire marks. Deciduous trees will retain conspicuous marks for a very long time. Particular care is needed with young branches, which grow fast.

Tilt-head wire cutters have a tilted head with which you can clip wire at the desired spot at any angle. They can also cut wire that has bitten into the bark.

A wire cutter with a long shank can easily access narrow and deep places.

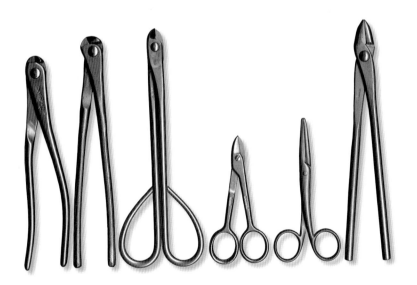

Wire cutters and wire pliers used for wiring. From left: a general-purpose wire cutter, a tilt-head wire cutter for unwiring, a wire cutter with a long shank, a mini wire cutter for thin wire, small wire pliers for applying and removing wire on branch ends, and general-purpose wire pliers.

Coiling wire around your finger, often recommended as a way of practicing wiring, is highly instructive. You should no more wrap the wire in such a way that it creases your finger and constricts the blood flow than wind it tightly around a tree, for trees are alive just on the exterior. This is likewise true for ancient trees that have grown to immense size. The outermost skin is the only living part of a tree.

Just underneath the bark is the vital cambium. As well as taking care not to scar the bark when wiring, you must keep an eye out so that the wires you have applied do not bite into the tree. The cambium becomes the site of active cell division during the season of growth; trees thicken not by fattening from the inside but by directly growing new tissue near the surface. At the same time, each year they accumulate a new layer of dead tissue in the interior in the form of a growth ring. In other words, the wood that comprises the growth rings is actually an aggregation of cells that have died away.

Because the growth of trees occurs on the exterior, or just under the wiring, wires will begin to bite in surprisingly fast. (Incidentally, although the wires are described as biting into the tree, the truth is that the tree grows outward to engulf the wires.)

Also located under the bark are sieve tubes, through which the sugars photosynthesized in the leaves are carried down to the roots. If wires obstruct this flow, the roots will soon weaken and the health of the entire bonsai will be impaired. The surface of the bonsai is thus highly delicate, so be heedful at all times that you do not damage the bark.

Wiring can be done at any time of the year, but deciduous bonsai are easiest to wire while they are leafless. If you wire a bonsai at the height of the budding season, meanwhile, you are likely to damage young buds and young leaves, whether the tree is deciduous or evergreen.

More critical is the question of when to remove the wire. Trees generally grow most vigorously in the period between late spring and the beginning of summer, as well as in early fall, when temperatures have dropped to comfortable levels and the days are still long. These are the times when wiring is particularly effective, but the danger of the wires biting into the bonsai will also be highest. The upper branches—which receive a lot of sunlight—and young branches grow particularly fast. I advise you to keep a close eye on these branches and to unwire early.

Training Thick Branches and Trunks

There are two instances in which training cannot be done by hand, even with the help of wire. The first is when the part you wish to correct is too thick to be bent manually, and the second is when you want to make a pinpoint adjustment that cannot be made accurately by hand, even though the branch or trunk may not be oversized.

Metal bars for bending (left), and jacks. Bending bars are available in a range of curvatures.

From left: Levers of three different sizes and an easy bending lever for the *satsuki* azalea.

Jacks and levers are used in such situations. In addition to giving you much enhanced power, these tools enable you to adjust a more precise section to a more precise degree than when using your hands. Moreover, by tactfully using two levers together, you can make subtle corrections quickly and at will.

USING BENDING TOOLS TO SHAPE BONSAI

Levers

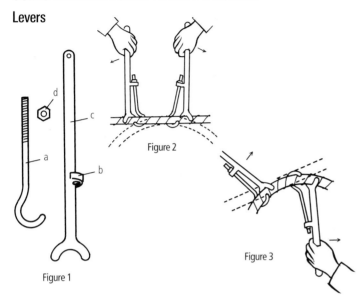

Figure 2

Figure 1

Figure 3

STEP 1. Wire the part of the tree that you will be bending or straightening. You will also need to wrap paper, cloth, or rubber around the wires and levers beforehand to prevent the bark from scarring.

STEP 2. Insert the hook (a) in figure 1 through the hole (b) in the handle (c). By turning the nut (d), adjust the length of the hook to a suitable length for clamping on the branch.

STEP 3. Firmly clamp the lever onto the branch and apply your strength to it to bend (figure 2) or straighten (figure 3) the branch to the desired position. By using not one but two levers, as in figures 2 and 3, you will be able to work with greater ease and precision. Using two levers is especially effective when the section you wish to adjust is narrow or when you want to make a curve with a small radius.

Jacks (with bending bars)

If a trunk is too sturdy to be bent or straightened with levers, you can use a jack together with a bending bar. Jacks can be applied to trunks of up to about 3 ¼ inches (8 cm) in diameter.

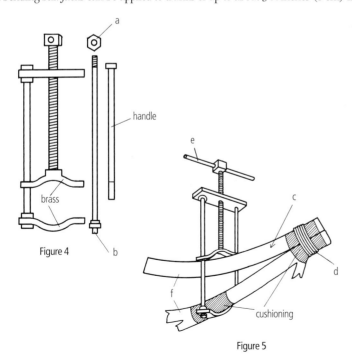

handle

brass

Figure 4

Figure 5

cushioning

STEP 1. Unscrew the nut (a) in figure 4 to take off the side rod (b). The jack is now ready to be put into place.

STEP 2. The bending bars (c) in figure 5 come in a variety of sizes and are curved to different degrees. Select a bar of suitable size for your bonsai and of the desired curvature, and attach one end to the tree with wire (d). To protect the bark, be sure to apply rubber or similar cushioning where the wire and the bar come in contact with the tree.

STEP 3. Adjust the distance between the clamps of the jack and slip the trunk and bar between them. In this position, reattach the rod removed in step 1 and assemble the jack. To keep the jack from sliding on the bar when it is tightened, fasten the two together with wire by utilizing the holes in the ends of the bar.

STEP 4. Insert the handle (e) through the hole at the head of the screw. Slowly and cautiously turn the handle to tighten the jack. Once you have bent or straightened the trunk to the desired angle, wire the other end of the bending bar to the tree at point (f).

STEP 5. Loosen the jack, then remove the rod as you did in step 1 and take the jack off the tree.

The bending bar is left on at this time. It should be removed along with the wire wrapped around the trunk, however, before the wire starts biting into the tree. Repeat the procedure if your bonsai has not yet attained the desired curve. If you apply too much force and break the tree, or if the wire bites into it, your efforts will come to nothing. Therefore, when you wish to bend or straighten a bonsai to an extensive degree, it is safer to train the tree gradually, in two or three stages, rather than trying to do it all at once.

From the Tree Doctor · Training Pruned Stems

A branch that has been skillfully pruned with the proper tools at the proper time will heal quickly, and the wounds will eventually become indiscernible. Care must be taken, however, when bending or straightening an area that was pruned in the past.

Traces of pruning will always remain with the tree to some extent, even though many years may have elapsed and the wound may appear on the surface to have healed cleanly. For all you know, there could be a cavity beneath a wound

that was slow to heal. At the very least, the pliancy of the wood where a tree was once pruned will differ from that of the rest of the tree. Such a part is more prone to giving in to the concentrated force that is applied when attempting to bend or straighten it. Moreover, it will be difficult to attain a natural curve.

Bear these points in mind when training your bonsai. At the same time, always strive to prune your branches appropriately, as pruning has lasting repercussions.

Sturdy trunks and branches can be bent with relative ease by first creating lengthwise splits in them with a trunk splitter.

The blades of a root cutter (left), and the blades of a trunk splitter. The two are designed for very different purposes and hence have blades of contrasting thickness and shape. Never use one for the purpose of the other; root cutters are for cutting, trunk splitters are for cleaving the trunk.

Using a Trunk Splitter

When correcting a bonsai on a more ambitious scale or when bending an extremely thick stem, that area is split lengthwise before being trained. Professional gardeners in Japan have traditionally employed this technique to fashion pines and other trees in the *moyogi* (informal-upright) style.

Trunks of up to about 2 inches (5 cm) in diameter can be split reliably and efficiently by using a trunk splitter, though other tools—like a wedge-shaped graving chisel—are sometimes used instead if the trunk is particularly large. Bonsai trunk splitters come in a range of sizes and have tapering, wedgelike blades. As their name suggests, they are designed to split trunks and create fissures. To use, close the blades of the trunk splitter until they bite into the trunk's core, then wiggle the handles up and down to split the trunk using leverage. Repeat this the necessary number of times at suitable intervals to create a continuous fissure.

Designed to be used in this manner, trunk splitters have thick, sturdy blades. Although root cutters and branch cutters have similarly opposing blades, their blades are thin and are fundamentally different from those of trunk splitters. For this reason, they cannot be substituted for the latter.

You may split the trunk in quarters or sixths, depending on its size and how far you wish to bend it. In either case, it is crucial that you make the splits accurately and evenly through the center. After the trunk is split, give the splitter a twist to widen the gap. To keep the twist from coming undone, firmly and closely wrap rope around the trunk. The rope will let air through while preventing drying. The trunk is fixed in place until it grows and stabilizes sufficiently in the new shape, its cambium fused and covered in a uniform surface layer.

The use of a trunk splitter in the bending procedure requires somewhat advanced skill. But with mastery, the creation of dynamically curved magnum opuses will be within your reach.

The powerful trunk splitter can also be used to effectively and efficiently make *jin* on the apex of the trunk or on thick branches.

From the Tree Doctor | Overreliance on Wiring

In the opening paragraph of the current chapter, my father speaks of "adjusting" or "altering" the shape of a bonsai. By wiring the tree or by using modern training tools, it is also possible to completely re-create its shape. As you have read in Chapter 2, however, my father advises against trying to force a bonsai into a shape that greatly deviates from the natural form of that species.

How far you go in this regard depends on your personal aesthetic values, but here are a few more points to consider. Relying too heavily on wiring to coerce a bonsai into a given shape can be highly problematic. When a bonsai has been trained over a short period by force, the shape may not only look unnatural but may be hard to maintain over an extended time. The plant is likely to lose its shape quickly once the wiring has been removed, and you will be obliged to keep falling back on wiring.

If you have shopped for bonsai, you have probably seen many specimens that are wired into what appear to be fine, standard bonsai shapes. I would hope that the readers of this book would avoid ready-made bonsai like these, but will choose to patiently craft bonsai for themselves by caring for the plants in an appropriate fashion based on a thorough understanding of the physiology of plants.

Wiring is a valid technique that can be beneficial in the process of cultivating bonsai. But I would ask you to remember one fact: even today, there are bonsai masters who never use wire and yet create beautiful specimens by regulating the growth of plants almost solely with shears. Find a path that meets your taste while respecting the natural tendency of the plants.

This natural-looking bonsai was grown from seed and shaped without the use of wires or any special equipment — only care and attention. Trident maple (*Acer buergerianum*), 30 years, 28 inches (70 cm).

CHAPTER 12

Making *Jin* and *Sharikan*

In nature, you may notice branches that have become bald and withered after breaking midway under the force of the wind or the weight of snow. Or you may see trunks that have turned bone white after being gouged, twisted, or bent by the impact of rocks that came tumbling down the hill. Trees with features like these are often collected from the wild and nurtured as *yamadori* bonsai.

When most of its bark has peeled off and all but a small amount of live tissue conveying water has withered to a bone white, the trunk is called *sharikan*. Bone-white deadwood on a branch, meanwhile, is called *jin*. *Sharikan* and *jin* not only impart the immense vital strength of wild trees that have survived years of harsh weather, but accentuate the trees' age. Specimens boasting well-executed *jin* and *sharikan* even seem to emanate an aura of divinity that transcends all else. In fact, the *kanji* character for *jin* literally means "divinity."

Artificially creating an awe-inspiring bonsai with *jin* features through the use of various tools to reproduce the image of aged trees in nature is an activity expert cultivators have performed for ages. For many general enthusiasts it is a challenge that they would like to take on at least once in their bonsai careers.

This sargent juniper (*Juniperus chinensis*), originally collected from the wild, has a magnificently twisted trunk with bone-white *sharikan* and *jin*. In the 1970s it was shipped from Japan to the Brooklyn Botanic Garden in New York, where it was carefully nurtured. Unfortunately, it died several years later. In honor of its extraordinary figure, today the tree is preserved at the garden. (Photographs by Masakuni Kawasumi II, 1970.)

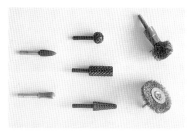

Various tools for a power drill or an electric rotary tool.

Graving chisels for drill or rotary.

Graving chisels with blades of varying widths.

Gravers with wooden grips, for light work.

All-steel gravers. As the handles and blades are made in one piece, all-steel gravers are suitable for heavy-duty work. The blades are variously shaped to allow easy carving of different parts of a tree.

Creating *jin* and *sharikan* effects is not at all difficult. It was once thought to require a lot of time and effort, because everything had to be done manually using a limited number of ordinary woodworking chisels and gravers. But today compact electric tools are easy to come by, and there is a rich selection of chisels and gravers made specifically for bonsai work, so that much time and effort can be saved.

Later in this chapter I demonstrate how to work with these tools; then you can try shaping your own bonsai into the likeness of a weathered wild tree. Once it has attained a more natural appearance through several years of love and care following the *jin*-making operation, the tree may possibly become an object of beauty that transports viewers to a suspended reverie of *wabi* (quiet refinement) and *sabi* (timeworn elegance).

Bonsai with exquisite *jin* and *sharikan* can only be made from conifers, such as the sargent juniper, which do not easily decay. *Jin* is not suitable for deciduous trees, as they are generally more prone to decay. The trunk of some deciduous trees, like the Japanese apricot, is sometimes carved, but this is to give it the appearance of having decayed through and through, turning it into a specimen with *sabamiki* (a split trunk). *Sabamiki* is another highly enjoyable bonsai form that expresses a tree's antiquity.

Creating a *sharikan* effect may be thought of as *jin*-making on a larger scale. Below I give some important precautions regarding trunk carving.

CAUTIONS BEFORE CARVING THE TRUNK

A bundle of *mizusui* runs from the base of each branch to the roots. The most important point when carving out a part—or the bulk—of the trunk's core is to identify the flow of the *mizusui* of each branch you intend to keep and to leave the tissue along that path covering at least the same width as the base of the branch. You should be able to identify the *mizusui* by closely observing the pattern of the bark and following it down from the base of the branch. I advise you to study the bark carefully before beginning to carve the trunk, as not all *mizusui* will run vertically up from the roots; in fact, some will appear to spiral around the trunk.

How to Make a *Sharikan*

The best tree for making a *sharikan* is a well-shaped specimen with a thick trunk. However, any conifer of reasonable size and fine disposition will serve your purpose. Here I use a young specimen, as young trees are relatively easy to procure. Even young trees can be made into presentable *sharikan* bonsai in the space of several years by carving them substantially and creating the basis for an elegant *sharikan* finish.

STEP 1. For our example, I use a sargent juniper (*Juniperus chinensis*) that has been field grown for 15 years. It has been tentatively potted for the procedure. The trunk has a circumference of 5 inches (13 cm) at the base and a length of approximately 39 inches (1 m). Although the branches are short, the tree is well foliated and has plenty of vigor, so it should be capable of withstanding the operation.

STEP 2. Before you begin carving the trunk, identify the paths of the lifelines, and mark which portions to carve. Do this carefully, as it is the most important step in determining your success.

STEP 3. It is time to begin carving. First, roughly shave off the surface with an electric chisel.

STEP 4. Shave the surface evenly, checking the overall balance so as not to work too heavily in any one area. Work with a blade of between ⅓ and ½ inch (9 to 13 mm), taking care not to shave off too much. If the blade is too wide, it can only be used on a limited area and will create more friction than is desired.

STEP 5. Using *jin* pliers, peel off the bark of the branches to be worked into *jin* and roughly make them into the intended shape. The finishing touches will be applied later, at the same time as they are applied to the trunk, at which point the branches should take on a natural look.

STEP 6. Roughly shave the surfaces of your target areas, such as around branch stems. Work cautiously using a ⅓ inch (9 mm) blade so as not to shave off too much.

STEP 7. Here is the tree after its surface has been roughly shaved with an electric chisel. For detailed work and hard-to-reach areas that cannot be worked on with an electric chisel, other electric tools or manual graving tools from the selection of tools introduced earlier are used.

STEP 8. Electric rotary tools can be used for semifinishing details that are hard to work on with electric chisels, for carving grooves, and for a range of other tasks.

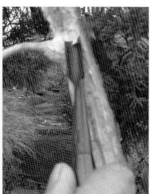

STEP 9. A variety of chisels and gravers are available for smoothing different parts of the tree with different demands. Select the tools accordingly to perform the finishing work. For example, a double-edged graver with a curved blade is highly useful for smoothing flat surfaces.

STEP 10. Cautiously smooth out the areas bordering the lifelines using an exceptionally sharp graver. This step is key in order that the lifelines may eventually spread and grow over the carved areas in a flawless manner.

STEP 11. The trunk is bent at this time, since this particular tree is not curved enough. Having just been carved, the trunk should be quite pliable. There are a variety of bending bars for shaping the trunk to different degrees. Select the appropriate bar for bending your tree, and with wire, secure one end of the bar to the part that will be bent. I have wrapped a rubber strip around the trunk to protect the bark. Although I have attached the bar at the lower end because some branches are in the way and because of the shape of the tree, the trunk will generally conform more closely with the shape of the bar if the bar is attached at the upper end, where the trunk is usually thinner.

STEP 12. A jack is attached to the other end of the bar with wire and tightened until the trunk has bent to the desired angle. Gently tighten the bolt little by little, taking care that the trunk does not break and that none of the tools come loose. Bending should be fairly easy, because the trunk has been winnowed down and, moreover, because the wood has not yet dried. I have clamped a hand vise onto the lower end of the bending bar to better secure it to the trunk. The jack is ordinarily kept on the tree for a while, but as a carved trunk is easily bent you can remove the jack in a fairly short time, after which the trunk can be held in place by wrapping it with thick wire. (For more detailed instructions, refer to the section on jacks in Chapter 11, Training and Reshaping.)

STEP 13. The curvature of the trunk is also adjusted or straightened at this time using two levers. By using a pair of levers, you can make precise corrections, even in a narrow section. Before applying the levers, I wired the area to be corrected. (See also the discussion on levers in the previous chapter.)

STEP 14. Once you have finished carving, apply undiluted lime sulfur to the carved surfaces. This will preserve the beautiful white color of the carved area over a prolonged period, as well as kill germs and prevent rotting. In some cases the solution is not applied until after the carved surface has naturally weathered, but if you perform the procedure in a warm season it is safer to apply the solution immediately.

STEP 15. The tree has now been replanted to face front, the carving and rough shaping of the trunk completed. Once the shapes of the branches have been adjusted with more wire, you will have the foundation of a *sharikan* bonsai. Avoid removing too many leaves at this point to allow the remaining lifelines to fatten swiftly. Undo the wires after your tree has recovered and stabilized, and patiently develop its form over a number of years.

How to Make *Jin* on a Branch or at the Apex

Dead and unnecessary branches can often be converted into *jin* by cutting them midway rather than at the base and peeling off the bark. Keep this possibility in mind when pruning.

The bark on the tip of a branch or on a branch that is ½ inch (1 cm) or less in diameter will come off easily by rotating a pair of *jin* pliers around the branch. Or you can shred off the bark in small pieces with the end of a tool.

Smooth surfaces can be swiftly peeled with a tool specifically designed for peeling bark, though gravers need to be used for intricate places.

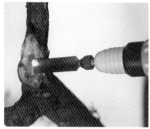 

Use electric tools on thick branches. Not just the bark, but also the woody tissue is carved until the branch is in proportion to the other *jin*.

Another way to visually age a tree is by peeling the bark around the apex of the trunk to simulate a treetop that has been struck dead by lightning. To craft a *jin* at the top of a thick trunk, use a trunk splitter.

From the Tree Doctor | About *Mizusui*

Mizusui, which literally means "water intake," is a popular term used in Japanese bonsai circles. But the actual paths of water from the roots—the vessels—run not along the surface of the tree but beneath it in the core wood. The bundles of *mizusui* you are identifying are actually bundles of sieve tubes, which convey the sugars produced in the leaves by photosynthesis. Although you cannot directly see the sieve tubes from the outside, you can observe their flow by looking closely at the bark, on which are marked the traces of growth. The expression "water intake" may give the impression that the flow of fluid begins at the roots and goes up the trunk, through the branches, and then to the leaves, but the actual course is from the branches to the trunk and, finally, to the roots. That is why you are being advised to follow the lines down, and why the width you leave must be equal to or greater than the branch's width at its base. As trees are alive just on the exterior, the sieve tubes running just under the surface can be thought of as the lifelines of trees. Trees will be able to survive as long as these paths are secure. Thus, leaving the lifelines fully intact is key to your success in creating *jin* and *sharikan*.

CHAPTER 13
Making *Ishitsuki* Bonsai

Bonsai that encompass a rock in their design are called *ishitsuki*. The types of *ishitsuki* bonsai are various: some are planted in hollows of natural rocks (photographs 1 and 2), some are planted atop thin slabs of rock that are either flat or slightly curved (photographs 3 and 4), while still others are planted in pots with exposed roots grasping carefully selected rocks (photographs 5 and 6). In all of these types the rock plays a central role in the composition, and these specimens are thus all called rock-grown bonsai.

When making an *ishitsuki* bonsai of the first kind, it is usual to plant several trees in separate hollows if it is an upright rock resembling a sheer cliff (photograph 2), and a single tree if the rock is low and wide (photograph 1). A thin slab is commonly used for

1. A *netsuranari* (sinuous root) bonsai of Japanese white pine planted in a hollow on the crest of a natural rock.

2. An *ishitsuki* bonsai of Japanese white pine planted in a hollow on the side of a natural rock.

3. A *yoseue* (group planting) of Japanese maple on a flat rock.

4. Japanese white pine in the *fukinagashi* (windswept style) planted on a curved sheet of rock.

5&6. An *ishitsuki* bonsai of trident maple with raised roots. The condition of the roots 50 years after planting.

crafting a *yoseue* (group planting) depicting a spacious landscape (photograph 3), though at times a single tree is planted instead. Solo planting is popular especially if the slab is curved (photograph 4). In any type of *ishitsuki* bonsai, it is important to achieve harmony between the rock and the tree—or trees—to maximize the beauty of both.

The greatest merit of *ishitsuki* bonsai in terms of cultivation is the fact that, unlike potted bonsai, they need not be replanted for many years. In potted bonsai, roots that have reached the edge of the pot will either turn back inward or run along the edge, eventually filling the pot's interior to cause root clogging. In an *ishitsuki* bonsai, meanwhile, root tips that extend out from the side or top of the soil—which occurs often because the amount of soil is small—will die off, having nowhere to go, and are replaced by the growth of fresh roots. *Ishitsuki* bonsai are constantly undergoing this cycle of root regeneration, making repotting unnecessary for a very long time. But a potted *ishitsuki* bonsai will need to be regularly repotted, just like other potted bonsai.

How to Make an *Ishitsuki* Bonsai with a Slab of Rock

Below I explain how to make an *ishitsuki* bonsai. I use a flat slab for our example.

STEP 1. What to prepare:

Flat rock A rock of the desired size. Here I use a rock measuring roughly 24 inches (60 cm) by 12 inches (30 cm).

Wire wire about ¹⁄₂₄ inch (1 mm) in diameter, for fastening the trees to the rock.

Wire cutter Always cut wire with a wire cutter and not with ordinary bonsai shears.

Instant glue For securing the wire to the rock. Choose a type that comes in a set with ceramic powder.

Scoop For scooping up soil.

Spray For preventing root dehydration while you work.

Trowel For smoothing out the topsoil.

Tweezers A type with a spatula on its head, for affixing moss on the topsoil.

Turntable The work will be done on a turntable.

Clay-rich soil For building a wall around the planting soil.

Planting soil Here I will use Japanese *akadama* soil with ⅛ inch (3 mm) grains, but you should select a soil that goes well with your chosen specimen, as discussed earlier.

Moss A small amount to dress the topsoil.

Seedlings It is best to have an odd number of plants.

STEP 2. The plants I use are Japanese maple (*Acer palmatum*) seedlings between 1 and 3 years from sprouting. Seedlings that have branches or roots only on one side, and hence cannot be planted solo, make good material for a group planting. The roots are generally not trimmed (unless they are spread out over an especially wide area). Rinse the roots and soak them in water until it is time to plant. Group plantings preferably comprise an odd number of trees.

STEP 3. Pour some ceramic powder where you will glue the wires in place.

STEP 4. Fold the wires in half. Holding the folded end of each wire against the rock, gather the ceramic powder around it and fix it in place by dripping instant glue over the powder and wire. Check that the agent has spread throughout the cement and that the rock and wire are securely glued together. Be careful not to get any of the agent in your eyes or on your hands.

STEP 5. The wires have been glued on. Leave the wires longer than you think will be necessary; the extra length can be cut off later. The number of wires is determined by the number of plants, as well as their size and placement. Use only as many wires as needed. The wires will get in the way of the roots' growth once the plant has taken root, so bear in mind that you will need to cut off the wires as soon as the trees have established themselves on the rock.

STEP 6. Knead the clayish soil well and roll it into narrow strips. With the strips build a wall to enclose the planting soil, pressing down firmly so that it sticks securely to the rock.

STEP 7. The wall of soil has been completed.

STEP 8. Pour planting soil (with grains of about ⅛ inch or 3 mm in this example) inside the wall. The soil should be well watered and properly drained beforehand. The moderately damp soil will keep the roots from drying quickly even if you take some time placing and planting the trees. The added weight also makes it convenient for planting the trees firmly.

STEP 9. The soil is now ready for planting. Note that it is a little higher toward the center than at the edges.

STEP 10. Begin planning the layout by tentatively planting the group of trees that will form the centerpiece. It will be easier to position them if you place the trees three at a time so as to form scalene triangles.

STEP 11. The positions of the three primary trees have been set. Do not fasten them with wire yet, so that you can make final adjustments later.

STEP 12. Position the trees of the second group, which will counterbalance the first, then position the trees of the third group. The overall composition is gradually determined in this manner. Lay the trees out using the principles of scalene triangles and odd numbers, while being mindful that the trunks of the trees should not overlap when viewed from the front.

STEP 13. Keep an eye on rootlets. If they begin to dry, hydrate by occasionally spraying them with water.

STEP 14. Fix the trees in place once you have finished positioning them all. Without fastening the trunk, lightly press down the spreading roots with wire. Make sure to apply the wires in such a way that they can be easily removed after the plants have taken root.

STEP 15. Small trees do not need to be fastened with wire but are held in place by the weight of the planting soil. Fasten a tree only when absolutely necessary.

STEP 16. After all the trees have been fixed in place, first press down the soil around the roots of each tree with a trowel. Next, press down and smooth out the entire topsoil. Be careful not to apply too much pressure when doing this.

STEP 17. The topsoil has been smoothed out, and the basic planting procedure is now finished.

STEP 18. Place moss on the topsoil. Tweezers are one of the most frequently used bonsai tools, and here the trowel-shaped end is used to guide the moss into position. The soil of *ishitsuki* bonsai generally dries a lot quicker than that of potted bonsai, and all the more so with those on flat rocks. Moss not only serves an aesthetic purpose but also helps prevent evaporation from the soil surface. In addition, it is highly effective in keeping the soil from being washed away during rain or watering.

STEP 19. The soil has been dressed with moss, and the bonsai has been completed. Immediately water the bonsai liberally to let the soil and plants settle down. Put the bonsai in a sunny place and keep it well watered while you wait for the trees to bud. If the weather is cold, make sure that the soil does not freeze. Do not prune the trees yet unless it is absolutely necessary. The trees will take root quickly, as the roots have not been cut like they ordinarily are when a tree is repotted. Observe the sprouting of the buds and trim them as you see fit, and feed diluted liquid fertilizer as needed.

Henceforth the bonsai is cared for in the same manner as other bonsai. Unless any of the plants wither or the trees grow out of proportion to the rock, you will not need to replant for quite a while.

An *ishitsuki* bonsai of Japanese maple after having been crafted in the method described above.

The same bonsai after 3 summers.

The same bonsai the following fall.

From the Tree Doctor | Caring for *Ishitsuki* Bonsai

The unwalled soil of an *ishitsuki* bonsai drains and ventilates very well, allowing the roots to breathe freely. And during the day the rock, which is easily warmed by the sun, makes the roots active by keeping them at a relatively high temperature. For these reasons, *ishitsuki* bonsai generally grow faster than potted bonsai. However, for the same reasons they also dry quickly, so you must be careful that the soil does not run out of water. In the photographs here, moss has been planted on the topsoil to slow down evaporation.

Take care where you place a planting when the rock is largely exposed, since the rock can grow dangerously hot under a scorching summer sun. Also, avoid watering such a bonsai during the heat of day, when there is a high probabil-

ity that the roots will be damaged. If you must do so for compelling reasons, such as if the soil has dehydrated or needs to be immediately cooled down, you must make sure to thoroughly lower the temperature by sprinkling plenty of water over the entire bonsai, including the rock.

As a general rule of thumb an *ishitsuki* bonsai does not need to be replanted for a long time, although there are exceptions. Over the long run, the soil may decrease or harden on the surface and lose its permeability and water retentivity. It is thus important to water the bonsai cautiously, as well as to closely observe the soil conditions and take appropriate measures, such as adding soil or boring holes in it to allow the water to penetrate the surface, as necessary.

CHAPTER 14
Daily Care

As you well know, bonsai subsist through photosynthesis. Always keep this fact in mind as you go about cultivating them. The tips I give in this section on the daily care of bonsai are closely linked to this basic principle.

Where to Put Your Bonsai

Although trees are highly adaptable, different species will inherently thrive in different environments. Some will demand plenty of sunlight while others will need little; still others will not fare well in the heat of summer, and so forth. For each species, try to find

Elevate bonsai in the summer sun.

Bonsai given some protection.

Bonsai in an enclosed area, where they can be quickly covered during inclement winter weather.

a location that best suits its preferences. Bonsai that have special needs, such as those recovering from recent surgery, preferably should be given sunny spots. If a bonsai likes cool places, you may need to shade it with a cloth or put it in an airy, elevated spot.

Small differences in the amount of sunlight or the temperature throughout the year can greatly affect the health and growth of your bonsai. By placing it wisely and taking advantage of the different conditions that each location offers, you will be able to broaden the choice of trees that you can rear out of doors.

Use turntables that are low and stable and will be weather resistant.

Turntables

Occasionally, bonsai need to be rotated. This is because, in the case of species that require a lot of sunlight, branches that are perpetually in the shade or receive less sunlight will weaken and, not infrequently, may die. Also, branches will generally grow in the direction of the sun.

Rotating bonsai will be easy if they are kept on turntables designed for the purpose of regulating sunlight exposure. These turntables are highly advantageous not only for improving the radiation balance but also for performing various daily tasks, such as watering, conducting health checks, bud trimming, and weeding.

Watering

Bonsai ordinarily are not watered until the topsoil is dry. When watering them, the water is sprinkled until all of the soil is evenly moistened. The water will linger near the surface if you use only a small amount of water in an attempt to be frugal, and the deeper roots will not develop or, even worse, may die back. If this occurs, the branches may die as well.

To regulate how much water a plant gets, change the frequency of watering and not the amount you give at one time. The best tactic, however, is to adjust the basic water retentivity of the soil at the time of repotting. If you use soil that does not hold a lot of water, only a small amount will remain in the pot regardless of how generously you water it. On the other hand, if you want to feed a bonsai plenty of water, you can plant it in water-retentive soil.

It is ideal if the soils of all of your bonsai are equally dry when you make your regular watering rounds.

Bonsai that have recently been repotted are easy to water, as the soil will absorb moisture well, but there is a trick to watering those with less-absorbent soil. First go around watering each of your bonsai lightly so that the water does not overflow from the topsoil; then make a second, third, and fourth round in the same manner. This method may seem tedious, but it will save water and time in the end.

Koshimizu, or immersion, is another excellent way of watering your bonsai: you soak the bottom of the pot in water and let the water filter through the soil via the drainage hole by capillary action. Immersion works well for bonsai that have thick trunks or widespread roots, as well as for those with soil that will wash away easily, for seedbeds in which tiny seeds have been sown, and for miniature bonsai.

Using a watering can will allow you to keep accurate track of how much water you are giving. A good watering can—one that has minute spray holes that produce a very fine and gentle shower—is perfect for delicate watering of miniature bonsai and seed-beds. Furthermore, it has been proven that by spraying with a copper watering can, the trace of copper ions that seep into the water will aid the growth of moss on the bonsai.

In principle you should water your bonsai every day at a given time and with a set frequency, but at times some flexibility is needed. There could be no better treat for your precious bonsai at the end of a hot summer day than water sprayed on the leaves from above, which will help them recover from heat stress.

Watering is the most basic and important aspect in the nurturing of bonsai. Through watering, you are daily showering your bonsai with love.

Fertilizing

In natural settings, organic matter—dead leaves, the droppings and carcasses of insects and animals—is constantly accumulating on the forest floor and decomposing, with the nutrients eventually being absorbed by trees through the roots. Trees in the forests, where this natural cycle is at work, do not need any fertilizer. But bonsai, which are replanted in fresh soil at regular intervals, must be fed some fertilizer for sustenance. Although the nutrients contained in the fertilizer are not the direct source of energy on which bonsai subsist, they are essential for the healthy and steady growth of the trees.

In general, I believe the best fertilizer for bonsai is the organic kind, being the nearest alternative to the natural cycle. Fertilizers come in either solid or liquid form, and solid types can also be dissolved in water for use as liquid fertilizer. Solid fertilizer is used by placing a small amount on the topsoil so that the nutrients slowly seep out as the plant is rained on or watered. It acts gradually and, therefore, over an extended period. Liquid fertilizer, which is directly applied to the soil, acts immediately. But its effect is short term, as it will be quickly washed away by water or rain.

Place a small amount of solid organic fertilizer along the edges or in the corners of the pot. Solid fertilizer can also be dissolved in water to make liquid fertilizer.

The two types of fertilizer are used for different purposes, but overuse must be strictly avoided in either case. Overfeeding can bring grave and unexpected results, such as root damage, enlarged leaves, and the abnormal growth of branches and unwanted shoots. While I have never heard of bonsai having died from lack of fertilizer, there are countless instances of bonsai that have either died or gotten out of shape because of overfeeding. When using liquid fertilizer, it is safest to dilute it to a lower concentration than prescribed. Similarly, when using solid fertilizer, place smaller-than-prescribed blocks in the corners of the pot so that they do not touch the trunk or roots.

By using a fertilizer can, you can apply liquid fertilizer in desired amounts without accidentally getting it on the leaves, even with a *yoseue* (group planting) or a bonsai in a small pot. Be sure to water your bonsai especially well after feeding, whether the fertilizer is solid or liquid.

Applying liquid fertilizer with a fertilizer can.

Weeding

Weeds will sprout on almost every bonsai that is kept outdoors. They will grow very quickly and will spread deep, hardy roots in no time if not removed. As soon as you notice them, remove them by the roots with tweezers while they are still young.

Tweezers are one of the most basic bonsai tools, and you should always carry a pair

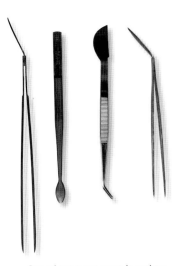

Bonsai tweezers come in various shapes and are used for many tasks, including placing and removing moss, smoothing soil, and pulling weeds.

with you on your daily rounds of the nursery. They are handy tools that can be used in various bonsai tasks, such as when applying moss or smoothing the soil.

Prevention of Disease and Insect Damage

Bonsai that are cultivated and maintained in good condition are well able to resist disease and repel insects. Your basic approach should be a preventative one: keep your bonsai in top condition and be alert to the first signs of weakness or pests.

Insects and germs have existed everywhere for hundreds of millions of years, and in nature, where the strong prey on the weak, the weak are inevitably threatened. Bonsai, too, will instantly become infested with insects or germs if they are weakened as a result of inadequate sun or water, inappropriate surgery, damaged cells having developed where a branch was pruned with a blunt tool, or other causes.

Although you may be tempted to rely on powerful chemical agents in such emergencies, you must always take care to consider the environment before using them. And to keep similar afflictions from recurring, it is essential that you accurately grasp the causes by reflecting on why the bonsai was infested with bugs or developed a disease.

Always take perfect care of your bonsai by paying attention to the basics, giving insects and diseases no chance to invade. Remember at all times that the strongest protection against disease and insect damage is daily care based on adequate sunlight and appropriate watering, as well as the relevant use of tools.

The kinds of insects and diseases that afflict trees are numerous and vary by country and region. I advise you to refer to texts on the subject published in your country to learn which trees are at risk from which pests, and in which season each pest is prone to strike.

Protection from the Weather

Even if you have been taking good daily care of your bonsai, they may suffer unexpected damage from extreme weather, such as long spells of rain or unusually low or high temperatures. Weather abnormalities have been reported worldwide in recent years, and bonsai cultivators need to keep a close eye on these phenomena. If you notice any signs of abnormal weather, swiftly carry out precautionary measures. Bonsai cultivation is not just about following conventions. At times you may need to drastically change your annual schedule, in anticipation of even the worst weather scenario.

CHAPTER 15
About Bonsai Tools

It is to be hoped that the demonstrations of bonsai techniques in chapters 4 through 13 have given you a full range of techniques for successfully cultivating bonsai, as well as a clear idea of the roles and functions of bonsai tools. The tools introduced in the demonstrations are just a few of the tools I make. (A complete catalogue may be found at www.masakuni.com.) A wide variety of other tools are involved in the year-round care of bonsai, and it would take several more volumes to discuss them in detail. In lieu of that, I will discuss some basic points regarding bonsai tools that you should find useful as you continue to enjoy bonsai cultivation for many years to come.

Start with the Essentials

It is best to start your collection of bonsai tools by purchasing those that you will use daily—one of each kind. The first tools you will need are a watering can and nozzle to water your bonsai every day, and tweezers to weed and clean your bonsai. Your first

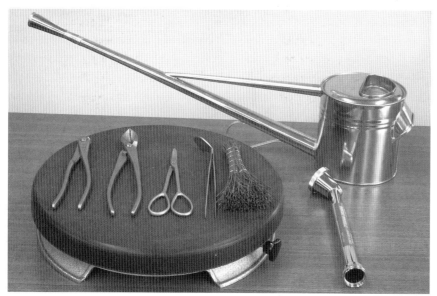

Tools for daily use, from left: wire cutter, concave branch cutter, bud-trimming shears, tweezers, broom, turntable, nozzle, and watering can.

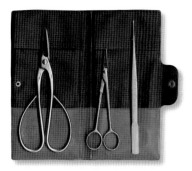 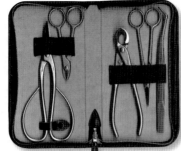 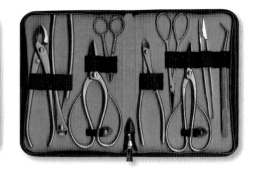

Bonsai tool sets of three, five, and nine pieces.

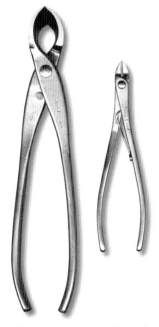

A branch cutter for trimming small branches measuring ⅛ inch (3 mm) in diameter or less (right) and a large concave branch cutter that can prune branches up to ⅝ inch (15 mm) thick.

shears should be bud-trimming shears with which you can reliably trim buds, one of the most important tasks. If you will be learning bonsai in an organized manner from the beginning of spring at a bonsai class, you will need a whole assortment of tools from the outset: a turntable, repotting tools, concave branch cutters and other pruning tools, tools for wiring, and so forth. Alternatively, you can buy a ready-made set of basic tools.

Once you have collected the basic tools, you will need to augment your toolbox according to the species of your bonsai and the tasks you wish to perform. Your repertoire of bonsai techniques will broaden as you obtain new tools: for instance, you can buy special-purpose tools and grow material for new bonsai by such methods as *toriki* (layering), *tsugiki* (grafting), or *sashiki* (growing cuttings), or you can try your hand at *jin* with an ample selection of chisels and gravers.

The Right Tool for the Right Task

While you will be purchasing additional tools according to your needs, many tools can be used for purposes other than that for which they are designed. There is no such thing, however, as all-purpose bonsai shears that can cut anything. Branches and wires come in all sizes, and the species and shapes of bonsai are diverse, as are the places to be cut. The lesser is not capable of serving for the greater, and in bonsai neither does the greater serve for the lesser. Always use a tool that is in keeping with your purpose: the right tool for the right task.

Notice the significant difference in the thicknesses of the blades of the wire cutter (left) and bud-trimming shears.

Shears (left) and concave branch cutters are held in this manner.

How to Hold Shears

Be sure to hold your shears correctly. By holding them the right way, you will be able to prune naturally, reliably, and stably without fatigue or unsteadiness.

How to Prune Branches

Use shears that require the least amount of exertion on your part. Cutting with the minimum strength is gentle on your hand as well as on the shears and will extend the life of the tool. At the same time, by cutting comfortably, you are being easy on the tree.

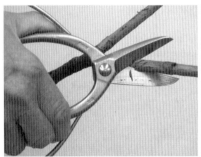

Cut at the base of the blade. Work as close to the base of the blades as possible when pruning branches. (For the delicate task of bud trimming, though, use the tip of the shears.) This is to make the most of leverage. For the same reason, in the case of a concave branch cutter, it is best to use the area of the blades that is closer to the fulcrum.

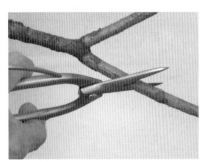

Cut at a slant. You can greatly reduce resistance by cutting the branch at a slight angle.

Cut in one action. Cut slowly and steadily, in a single action, without hesitation. Do not pause in the middle or twist the shears sideways, as blades are weakened by lateral force. Think of letting the shears do the cutting instead of trying to cut with brute force.

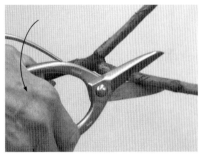

Rotate the blade slightly downward as you cut, using your whole body rather than just your arm. Thick branches are easier to prune if you draw the blade toward you as you cut. When using shears, apply your whole body to it rather than cutting with just your hands. This will allow you to work with stability and great ease, without straining the shears.

AFTER-USE CARE

Blades with well-sharpened edges cut well, as the applied force is effectively focused on the edges. Shears are designed to concentrate the force of the two blades along a single line, so it is important that the blades meet perfectly.

Sap will get on the back of the blades when you cut plants, and the performance of your shears will greatly diminish once the sap accumulates. It will come off easily if wiped immediately after use with a cloth that has been dampened and wrung out well. It will become stubborn once it has hardened, so I advise you to get into the habit of removing the sap as soon as you finish using the tool and always keep the blades—especially the back side—clean.

Rust is another detriment to blades. Lightly coat the blades with oil after you have thoroughly wiped off the sap to prevent rusting. Oil also decreases friction between the blades. Be sure to oil the hinge as well; applying just a single drop of oil on the hinge will keep the shears working well and dramatically improve their life span.

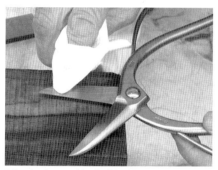
Wipe the front and back of the blades to remove sap and other material.

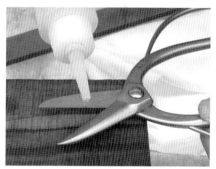
Apply a light coat of oil to the blades after each cleaning.

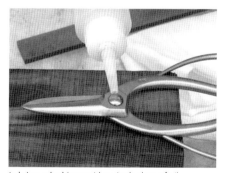
Lubricate the hinge with a single drop of oil.

MAINTAINING THE EDGE

It is the fate of any edged tool to become dull with repeated use. Cutting with a blunt tool is painful for the bonsai and stresses both the hand and the tool, as it causes greater friction. You also risk unforeseen accidents and injuries by trying to cut forcibly with dull blades.

Once the blades have been badly blunted, they will take a long time to sharpen, and in some cases you may need to take them to a specialist. But there is a good, easy way of maintaining their edge: lightly hone them while they are still sharp. This is the key— since the blades are still sharp, you hardly need to think of sharpening them; you need only lightly and briefly apply a whetstone against them. You can buy whetstones with which you can easily maintain the edge on your tools.

Below I explain the sharpening procedure.

SHARPENING SHEARS

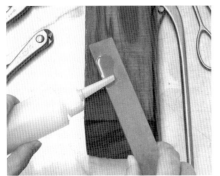

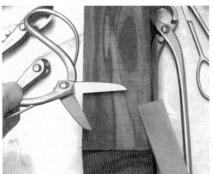

STEP 1. Apply oil (mineral based or petroleum based) to the whetstone. Oil prevents clogging of the whetstone and maintains its effectiveness. Oils with lower viscosity, such as petroleum-based oils, are generally less likely to clog the whetstone and will improve its effectiveness.

STEP 2. The outside of the blade is sharpened first. Open the shears and firmly hold one of the blades at an angle against a suitable base, such as a block of wood. You can sharpen by applying the whetstone flat against the beveled surface of the blade, but I recommend working at a larger angle so that it reliably meets the edge. The appropriate angle is between 25 and 30 degrees—a more acute angle for keenness and a less acute angle for strength.

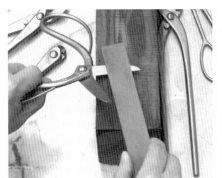

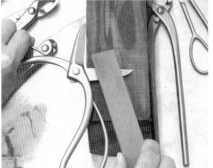

STEP 3. At a steady angle, slowly slide the whetstone away from you and toward the tip of the blade. Repeat this several times. Work gently and patiently; pressing too strongly in haste to sharpen the blade may influence the angle of the blade or lead to an accident. Just a few strokes will do if the blades have not yet become dull.

STEP 4. When the outside is well sharpened, a slight burr will occur on the inside. It will be hardly visible to the naked eye if you are sharpening the blade only lightly. To shave off the burr, place the whetstone against the inside of the blade and slide it away from you, using just the weight of the whetstone. Be sure not to put your strength into it; think of gently coaxing off the burr, rather than grinding it off. Oversharpening the inside of the blade will greatly reduce its edge.

NOTE: All the bonsai tools shown in the pictures can be honed with this whetstone.

SHARPENING BRANCH, KNOB, AND ROOT CUTTERS

When sharpening branch cutters, knob cutters, and root cutters, do as follows using the same whetstone and the oil utilized for the shears.

By using this whetstone, you will be able to keep most of your bonsai tools sharp over a long time.

Just as we regularly watch our health and protect ourselves against illness, it is important to keep an eye on the condition of your tools. Tools with blades should be handled, used, and sharpened with caution.

SHARPENING BRANCH, KNOB, AND ROOT CUTTERS

STEP 1. Carefully inspect the edges of the blades. The blades of branch cutters and similar tools will become misaligned. You will be able to clearly feel this by gently touching the tips with your finger. Make a note of how large the difference is.

STEP 2. The blade that crosses over the other is called the upper blade, and the one underneath it is called the under blade. (The branch cutter is turned over in the picture, so the blade that you see on top is the under blade.) The outside of the under blade is sharpened first. The blade is narrow at the tip; apply the whetstone flat against this part of the blade. As with shears, just a few light strokes are enough. Next, carefully shave off the burr on the inside of the blade.

STEP 3. The upper blade is sharpened with the blades closed. Place the whetstone against the narrow part of the blade and hone it the same amount as the level difference that you noted in step 1. When you have finished the outside, shave off the inside burr.

NOTE: After repeated sharpening, the blades eventually will become short and no longer meet. When the blades have become too short, you can adjust the distance between them by filing down the part of the stopper that touches the shank until the tips meet again.

Selecting Good Tools

The pleasure and peace of mind gained in bonsai cultivation is inextricably linked to the ease with which you can execute your ideas and the techniques introduced in these pages. The tools to choose are those that enhance and deepen these feelings, for that is what distinguishes genuinely good tools. The state of spiritual wealth that is achieved by using good tools and achieving good results is of utmost importance for growing fine bonsai.

Make sure to choose quality beginner's tools. Sharpness, durability, and reliability are basic qualities you should seek. Tools for beginners in the true sense are those that intensify your pleasure in bonsai. They can be used easily and with a natural fluidity to achieve good results. This will lead you to higher levels of skill.

Tools that can be used comfortably from the start will continue to serve more advanced needs as the user's skill improves, will transcend all differences of skill, and, at the end of the day, will prove to be the greatest money saver.

"Bonsai will be what they will be."

These are the words of one eminent bonsai master. What do you think of them? Do they impress you as a positive statement, or as a negative one with a tinge of resignation? To wrap up my comments as a tree doctor, I would like to give some thought to these words.

I believe there are two important notions that must be kept in mind at all times when cultivating bonsai. The first is that "bonsai are just the same as trees growing in nature," and the second is that "bonsai are entirely different from trees growing in nature." Both ideas are self-explanatory, and appear to contradict each other. Be that as it may, you will not do well in bonsai cultivation if your awareness of either notion is lacking.

Bonsai have the same basic properties and characteristics as their wild counterparts of the same species, whether we look at the shapes of the leaves and flowers, the amount of water and light needed, the preferred temperatures, or the manner of growth.

Meanwhile, being reared in pots of limited size, bonsai need our help. For one thing, bonsai need to be watered by hand, for they cannot possibly subsist on rain alone. And because their branches and roots will grow, albeit to a lesser degree than those of their wild counterparts, they must undergo a variety of procedures—including bud trimming, pruning, training, and repotting—in order to attain the right size and shape. In this sense, bonsai are different from their wild cousins.

But artificial though they are, bonsai do not submit entirely to our will when we seek to shape them. This is because the inherent properties of their species and the basic physiology of plants exert influences.

When giving a bonsai water or sunlight, you must have a good grasp of the preferences of that species, and when trimming buds or pruning branches you need to know how branches of that species grow. If the shape you envision departs greatly from the natural form of the species, the bonsai will not survive over the long term.

Thus, the sameness and difference of bonsai when compared with their wild cousins are inseparably linked. In fact, achieving a perfect balance between the two is essential to successful bonsai cultivation. In musical terms, they might be compared to the left and right hands in a piano composition written in counterpoint. In counterpoint the two melodies have equal weight, and one must not be stronger or weaker than the other. The famous Two-Part Inventions by Johann Sebastian Bach, which every beginner piano student practices, are apt examples.

As you approach the art of bonsai with an awareness of both concepts, an important key is the correct understanding of photosynthesis—the most fundamental principle of tree physiology. The method or course that you should take will reveal itself of its own accord if you look at every aspect of bonsai cultivation in terms of photosynthesis.

During the day, green leaves manufacture sugars by photosynthesis. Leaves are the only organs in a tree that produce energy, and the sugars they produce are analogous to the income of a household. Meanwhile, the live cells of a tree—including those of the leaves—are constantly breathing, just as we are. Energy is used in the process of breathing; this is analogous to the expenditure of household funds. A tree will be able to live if its income is greater than its expenditure, and the surplus can then be saved up. These savings are what finance the growth of the tree.

The subsistence and growth of a tree are thus determined by the balance between the income and expenditure of energy. Carbon dioxide is always present in the air, but light, water, and the temperature also play decisive roles in the photosynthetic process, so a tree's productivity will fall if there is not enough sunlight or water, or if the temperature is low. It follows that if you want your bonsai to grow, you should water it amply, give it plenty of sunlight, refrain from trimming the leaves, and keep it in an optimum temperature. If you wish to suppress its growth, on the other hand, you can do the opposite.

By thinking from the standpoint of securing adequate sunlight, you should be able to picture what you need to do when trimming buds, pruning branches, or shaping your bonsai. Doing so will similarly guide you in watering, placing, and repotting your bonsai, and it will further enable you to make rational, strategic choices.

There is one more key point in bonsai cultivation, and that is the correct use of good tools, which has been discussed throughout this book. Well-chosen tools will be your constant ally, give you confidence, and allow you to work with precision.

Now, let's return to the words, "Bonsai will be what they will be." Once you come to understand the relationship of the two seemingly opposed ideas mentioned at the beginning of this discussion, you will see that the statement is a positive one, with broad and profound implications. By caring for your bonsai with a proper awareness of its needs and nature's tendencies, your understanding of the trees will deepen and the way forward will present itself.

These words, it seems to me, illuminate the way to even more profound places. It is up to each of you to progress further along that path.

It was the spring of 2000, on the brink of the twenty-first century, when my father announced to me, as I helped him repot his bonsai, "I'll be writing a new book about bonsai soon, so I want you to offer your advice as a tree doctor." Before long, we had decided on the basic plan and our individual responsibilities. We began working on the book that very spring, adding new photographs from season to season. Then, in the summer of 2002, my father suddenly passed away, leaving behind an unfinished manuscript and the many bonsai that he had been growing for years.

On the same day that he suffered a stroke, my father, being no longer able to speak clearly, scribbled a note with a shaking, struggling hand. It read, "Leave the manuscript as it is." On his desk were an almost finished draft, some photographs, and a file of documents that he had left open. A publication schedule had already been set. He must have intended to get back to work immediately and hasten the book's completion. But that night my father slipped into a coma, and he never woke up again. He passed away eleven days later.

I assumed the name of Masakuni III and, with it, full responsibility for the completion of this book. Now on my own, however, the editing work took me longer than I had expected, and the fifth spring has arrived since the book's conception.

During the course of the book, many people have made contributions. Many of the masterpieces shown here were photographed at the Kyukaen nursery in the Bonsai Village in Saitama. We have been indebted to Kyukaen for about eighty years, or three generations, since my grandfather's time. Isamu Murata, who has inherited the nursery from his late father, the eminent Kyuzo Murata, gave me warm encouragement, as did his family, in addition to a wealth of thought-provoking advice. I have been supported as well by the kindness of many friends and acquaintances both in and outside of Japan. Most of all, I am grateful beyond words for the efforts of Barry Lancet, Tetsuo Kuramochi, and Nobuko Tadai of Kodansha International, who participated in the book from its planning and cheered me on to the last. My sincere thanks go also to Kay Yokota, who gladly took on the task of translating the manuscript, and to Yasuo Saji, who endured hours at a stretch of scorching sun or cold weather to shoot photographs for the book. Last, I would like express my gratitude to the designers, Kazuhiko Miki and Masumi Akiyama.

The following is an afterword that my father wrote at the time he finished the first draft. I would like to close this book, being as it is of my father's conception, with his own words. May his passion for bonsai reach the hearts of bonsai enthusiasts worldwide.

Masakuni Kawasumi III

Bonsai are adorable.

At the same time, though, bonsai have a vocal, assertive side. "I want some more water," they will insist, or, "I'd like to grow this branch on my right side out a bit longer." My bonsai flood me daily with protests like these as I make my regular rounds of the nursery.

If I were to comply with every one of their requests, they would not grow into fine bonsai. At times the cultivator must have his way. You must not raise your bonsai indulgently, but must take to them with some severity.

Cultivating bonsai is in some ways very much like child rearing. You must not give them too much or too little, neither too much water, nor too little. Water sprouts are prone to grow if you feed bonsai too much fertilizer, potentially disfiguring them. Leaving bonsai to their own devices, meanwhile, is all the more to be avoided. It is essential that you rein in their demands and strive to achieve moderation in everything.

Constantly watch over your bonsai with love, and you will be able to clearly make out what they are saying and to exploit the natural features of each tree.

It is my hope that this book will aid enthusiasts across the world in their endeavors to create splendid bonsai.

Masakuni Kawasumi II

APPENDIX
Japanese Bonsai Soil Types

Most of the major soils used in Japan, with the exception of regular river and mountain sand, are exported worldwide and should be readily available at a local bonsai store. Meanwhile, I have also seen similar soils in various parts of the world on my numerous trips overseas. For your reference, I basically make sole use of *akadama* soil for most species. I have had no difficulties growing bonsai with this soil, as I take close care of the plants by regularly repotting them, feeding them at appropriate intervals, watering them on a daily basis, and so forth. Below I introduce the primary types of soil that are used in Japan today for growing bonsai.

Akadama soil

Akadama tsuchi, widely known overseas as *akadama*, is the most commonly used soil in Japan. It is inorganic volcanic soil from Mt. Fuji and, at pH 6.5–6.8, leans very slightly to the acidic side. *Akadama* literally means "red ball," but the soil is actually ocher. It consists of fine pumiceous lava fragments that have consolidated into balls or grains. The soil scores high in both water retention and ventilation, owing to the minute holes and angular edges of the grains. There are also baked variations, called *yaki akadama tsuchi*, that have been fire hardened to enhance these qualities.

Kanuma soil

Kanuma *tsuchi* is a pale yellow soil consisting of weathered pumice emitted from the Mt. Asama volcano. The innumerable pores in the grains serve as reservoirs that hold over 20 percent more water than *akadama*, while the gaps occurring between the grains make for highly efficient ventilation. With an acidic pH value of 5.6–6.4, Kanuma soil is widely used as the ideal soil for *satsuki* azaleas.

Kiryu sand

Kiryu *suna* is a brownish yellow mountain sand extracted in the Kiryu area of Gunma Prefecture. It is harder than Kanuma *tsuchi* and holds and drains water well. Rarely used alone, it is ordinarily mixed into *akadama* soil at a ratio of 2:8 or 3:7 for use with pines. The pH value is a mildly acidic 6.5.

WATER RETENTIVITY OF JAPANESE SOILS   Research by Masakuni Kawasumi III

SOIL TYPE	Grain diameter (inch/mm)	Dry weight (oz/g)	Weight 30 min. after watering (oz/g)	Water retentivity (oz/g)	Water retentivity over weight (%)	Water retentivity compared to *Akadama* A
Akadama A	$^3/_{24}$–$^1/_{24}$ (3.0–1.0)	23.3 (660)	33.9 (960)	10.6 (300)	45	1.00
Akadama B	$^5/_{24}$–$^4/_{24}$ (5.0–4.0)	22.9 (650)	31.7 (900)	8.8 (250)	38	0.83
Kanuma	$^3/_{24}$–$^1/_{24}$ (3.0–1.0)	11.6 (330)	24.7 (700)	13.1 (370)	112	1.23
River sand A	$^2/_{24}$ (2.0)	49.4 (1,400)	58.2 (1,650)	8.8 (250)	18	0.83
River sand B	$^1/_{48}$ (0.5)	52.9 (1,500)	65.3 (1,850)	12.3 (350)	23	1.17

* Comparisons were made using 1.8 pints (1,000 cc) of each soil.

Fuji sand

Fuji *suna* is weathered lava from Mt. Fuji in the form of black sand. It is usually thinly sprinkled over the topsoil for decoration after a plant has been repotted, or occasionally mixed with *akadama* soil for such purposes as heat absorption. In addition to enhancing the beauty of the bonsai, dressing the topsoil with Fuji sand is believed to promote the emergence of young roots, as it improves the absorption of heat from the soil surface.

Granite sand

Granite sand is fine mountain sand formed by the perennial cycle of water filling fissures in the granite, then expanding as it freezes in winter and causing the granite to crack. It has been proven highly effective in growing long rootlets, as the gaps that occur between the coarse and sharp-edged grains ensure adequate drainage and ventilation. In western Japan, pine bonsai in training are usually cultivated solely in granite sand; *akadama* soil is rarely used.

River sand
Some cultivators mix a small amount of regular river sand in the planting soil to improve drainage. In principle, coarse grains of at least $\frac{1}{12}$ inch (2 mm) should be used for such purposes.

Sea sand is not used, as the salt content is difficult to remove even by washing.

Regular mountain sand
Mountain sand can be found in mountainous areas around the world. Recommended are coarse-grained varieties, among which porous types that retain water well are particularly favored.

For more details about water retention, see the discussion on soil in Chapter 8.

LIST OF TREES

ENGLISH	JAPANESE	LATIN
Beech	Buna	Fagus crenata
Camellia	Tsubaki	Camellia japonica
Chinese hackberry	Enoki	Celtis sinensis
Crape myrtle	Hyakujikko	Lagerstroemia indica
Cryptomeria (Japanese cedar)	Sugi	Cryptomeria japonica
Ezo spruce	Ezomatsu	Picea jezoensis
Horse chestnut	Tochinoki	Aesculus hippocastanum
Japanese apricot	Ume	Prunus mume
Japanese black pine	Kuromatsu	Pinus thunbergii
Japanese cypress	Hinoki	Chamaecyparis obtusa
Japanese judas tree	Katsura	Cercidiphyllum japonicum
Japanese maple	Yama-momiji	Acer palmatum
Japanese red pine	Akamatsu	Pinus densiflora
Japanese white pine	Goyomatsu	Pinus parviflora
Longleaf pine	Daiosho	Pinus palustris
Maple, type of	Hana-kaede	Acer pycnanthum
Maple, type of	Hinauchiwa-kaede	Acer tenuifolium
Oriental bittersweet	Tsuru-umemodoki	Celastrus orbiculatus
Persimmon	Kaki	Diospyros kaki
Sargent juniper	Shimpaku	Juniperus chinensis
Satsuki azalea	Satsuki	Rhododendron indicum
Spindle tree, type of	Nishikigi	Euonymus alatus
Star jasmine, type of	Teika-kazura	Trachelospermum asiaticum
Tamarisk	Gyoryu	Tamarix chinensis
Trident maple	To-kaede	Acer buergerianum
Wax tree	Haze	Rhus succedanea
Weeping cherry	Shidare-zakura	Prunus Itosakura
Weeping willow	Yanagi	Salix babylonica
Zelkova	Keyaki	Zelkova serrata
——	Iigiri	Idesia polycarpa
——	Isozansho	Osteomeles anthyllidifolia